VISUAL™
Quick Tips
Crochet

D1203827

VISUAL™
Quick Tips
Crochet

Visual®

by Cecily Keim and Kim P. Werker

BICENTENNIAL
1807
WILEY
2007
BICENTENNIAL

Wiley Publishing, Inc.

Crochet VISUAL™ Quick Tips

Copyright © 2007 by Wiley Publishing, Inc., Hoboken, New Jersey. All rights reserved.

Published by Wiley Publishing, Inc., Hoboken, New Jersey

For general information on our other products and services or to obtain technical support please contact our Customer Care Department within the U.S. at (800) 762-2974, outside the U.S. at (317) 572-3993 or fax (317) 572-4002.

Wiley also publishes its books in a variety of electronic formats. Some content that appears in print may not be available in electronic books. For more information about Wiley products, please visit our web site at www.wiley.com.

Library of Congress Control Number: 2007921828

ISBN: 978-0-470-09741-0

Printed in the United States of America

10 9 8 7 6 5 4 3 2 1

Book production by Wiley Publishing, Inc. Composition Services

Wiley Bicentennial Logo: Richard J. Pacifico

Praise for the VISUAL Series

Credits

Acquisitions Editor
Pam Mourouzis

Project Editor
Suzanne Snyder

Copy Editor
Elizabeth Kuball

Editorial Manager
Christina Stambaugh

Publisher
Cindy Kitchel

Vice President and Executive Publisher
Kathy Nebenhaus

Interior Design
Kathie Rickard
Elizabeth Brooks

Cover Design
José Almaguer

Photography
Matt Bowen

About the Authors

Cecily Keim documents her adventures in life, crocheting, and other creative endeavors at SuchSweetHands.com. Throughout her life, regardless of the type of study or type of job, making things has always fascinated Cecily. Her great-grandmother, Mama Mac, taught her to crochet at age 9. Since then crochet has become a favorite technique in her crafty arsenal. Cecily is mesmerized by the endless possibilities of crochet and loves passing on her enthusiasm as a writer, designer, and teacher. She teaches crochet classes and contributes her designs to magazines and books. She has also demonstrated her designs on the DIY channel's *Knitty Gritty* and *Uncommon Threads.*

Cecily lives in Los Angeles, watches too much television, and loves candy, her cats, and her boyfriend.

Kim P. Werker is the editor of *Interweave Crochet* magazine. She is also the founder and Creative Director of CrochetMe.com, the online crochet community for innovative patterns, tips, and tutorials, and a playground for meeting crocheters from all over the world. After a couple of earlier flings, Kim got back into crochet in 2004. She is a professional member of the Crochet Guild of America and The National NeedleArts Association, and travels throughout North America to teach about crochet and to meet enthusiastic crocheters. She has appeared on the television show *Uncommon Threads* and will appear on the PBS shows *Shay Pendray's Needle Arts Studio* and *Knit & Crochet Today.* She was thrilled to work again with Cecily on this follow-up to their first book, *Teach Yourself VISUALLY Crocheting.* Kim's other books include *Crochet Me: Designs to Fuel the Crochet Revolution* (Interweave Press, 2007), *Get Hooked,* and *Get Hooked Again* (Watson-Guptil 2006 and 2007, respectively).

Originally from New York State, Kim lives in Vancouver, British Columbia, with her husband and their dog. When she's not crocheting, writing, editing, or traveling, she enjoys reading, hiking, knitting, and playing in the garden.

Instructional Videos Online

We've filmed videos of a few of the techniques described in this book—just look for the symbol. To view the videos, go to www.wiley.com/go/crochetvqt.

Acknowledgments

We are greatly indebted to the people at Wiley who have made this book possible: Pam Mourouzis and Suzanne Snyder, who provided patience and guidance, always with kindness and humor; Cindy Kitchel, who expanded her crochet skills and showed them off so perfectly; and Matt Bowen, our photographer—all their efforts truly make this book special.

Cecily is grateful to have such a supportive and inspiring circle of friends and family, all willing to listen to her chatter on about crochet. Her biggest thanks go to Rob, who still believes it when she promises she will get the yarn collection under control.

Kim thanks her family and friends for being patient during her long absence from their lives while this book was in production. Especially to Greg, who truly had to live through it with her.

We are grateful to the Craft Yarn Council of America for their permission to reprint information about industry standards and for the tireless efforts they make to promote and document crochet.

Finally, to the crocheting community: We thank you for your enthusiasm for the craft and for your unending desire to learn more about it.

Table of Contents

Basic Stitches 26

Beyond the Basic Techniques 88

6

Finishing   134

7

Working from Patterns   160

chapter **1**

Hooks and Yarn

Before you start crocheting, take some time to familiarize yourself with the tools that will help you along the way. Starting a project with the right tools on hand saves time. In this chapter you'll find information to help you choose an appropriate hook for a project as well as suggestions for choosing, caring for, and winding yarn.

Hooks

SHAPE

Crochet hooks are generally 5 to 7 inches long. There is a hook at one end, which you use to grab yarn or thread and pull it through the stitches of your work. You hold the hook along its shaft.

Manufacturers shape their hooks differently. The sharpness or bluntness of the hook's point varies, as does the hook's depth. Try out a few brands until you find the shape you think works best.

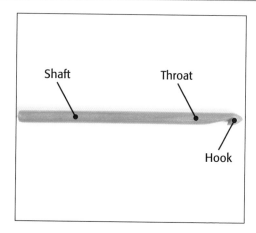

Shaft   Throat

Hook

HOOK COMPOSITION

Plastic hooks are usually hollow and lightweight. Most very large hooks are made of plastic. Metal hooks can be very smooth, enabling the yarn to slide with little resistance. Wood or bamboo hooks provide a bit of friction, which comes in handy when you're crocheting with slippery yarns.

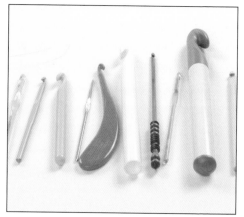

When using a wood or bamboo hook, rub the hook with a piece of wax paper to make the yarn slide more smoothly.

Some hooks are designed with a thick rubber handle to be easier to grip. Some hooks feature embellishments on the handle, but these are purely decorative.

OTHER KINDS OF HOOKS

Tunisian crochet hooks are longer than standard crochet hooks. This extra length allows the hook to hold many stitches, much like a knitting needle does. (See page 92 for more on Tunisian crochet.)

There are also double-ended crochet hooks made for a technique called *double-ended crochet* or *crochet on the double*.

Hook Sizes

Hook size is determined by the diameter of the hook's shaft. Hook size is marked differently in the United States, the United Kingdom, and the rest of the world.

Hook sizes in the United States and United Kingdom are marked by an arbitrary letter or number, respectively. Manufacturers often use slightly different labels for the same size hook, however. Hooks are most consistently labeled by the metric measurement of their diameter, which is an objective label. There is a growing effort to standardize sizes by using metric measurements only.

TIP

Small hooks make small stitches; large hooks make large stitches. Switching hooks will change the look and feel of the fabric you crochet.

DECIDING WHICH HOOK SIZE TO USE

Most yarn labels suggest a hook size to use; most patterns also list a recommended hook size. You may need to change hook size in order to match the gauge listed in a pattern or to achieve a pleasing drape and feel. Matching the gauge of a pattern is more important than using the exact hook size listed. In some instances, a yarn label provides only a recommendation for a knitting needle size. In this case, use a hook that matches or is slightly larger than the metric size.

DETERMINING A HOOK'S SIZE

If you're unsure of a hook's size because it is old or the label has worn off, you can use a hook gauge to measure it. The size indicated beside the smallest hole that the shaft of the hook fits into is the size of your hook.

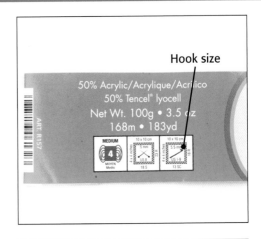

Hook size

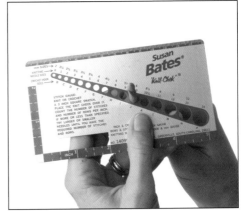

Compare Hook-Size Labels

HOOK SIZES

This chart lists equivalent crochet-hook sizes.

Hook Sizes		
Metric Size (in mm)	U.S. Size	U.S. Knitting-Needle Size
2	A	0
2.25	B	1
2.75	C	2
3.25	D	3
3.5	E	4
3.75	F	5
4	G	6
4.5		7
5	H	8
5.5	I	9
6	J	10
6.5	K	10½
8	L	11
9	M/N	13
10	N/P	15
15	P/Q	19
19	S	35

STEEL-HOOK SIZES

Steel hooks have a narrow shaft and tiny hooks intended for use with thin crochet threads to make finer lace and doilies. This chart lists equivalent sizes of steel hooks.

Steel-Hook Sizes	
Metric Size (in mm)	U.S. Size
0.75	#14
0.85	#13
1.0	#12
1.1	#11
1.3	#10
1.4	#9
1.5	#8
1.65	#7
1.8	#6
1.9	#5
2.0	#4
2.1	#3
2.25	#2
2.75	#1
3.25	#0
3.5	#00

Besides these tools, a sharp pair of scissors or a yarn cutter is useful. Keep these notions in a small case or kit so you always have them handy.

MEASURING TAPE

Use a measuring tape to take body measurements before you begin to crochet a garment. A measuring tape also comes in handy when checking gauge (see Chapter 7) and to keep track of your progress on a project. Measure your work frequently to make sure everything is going as planned.

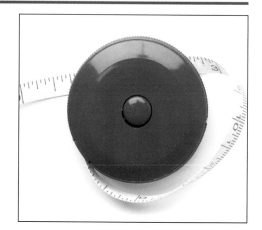

HOOK GAUGE

The hook-gauge holes help you to determine the size of an unmarked hook. (See the section "Compare Hook-Size Labels" on page 8.)

Note: Using the L-shaped window of hook gauges such as this one doesn't work well with certain textured stitches like bobbles and shells. To measure your gauge in these stitches, use a ruler or tape measure.

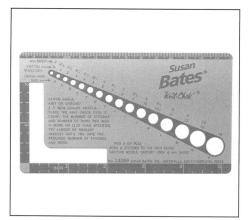

STITCH MARKERS

Stitch markers are useful in many situations. For example, when working in the round (see Chapter 3), you can mark the beginning of the round by placing a marker in the first stitch. You can buy stitch markers designed for this purpose or improvise with scraps of yarn or even earrings. When crocheting a garment, use stitch markers to indicate the placement of increases and decreases for shaping (see Chapter 3). Stitch markers are like a breadcrumb trail: Use them whenever you need to keep track of what you're doing.

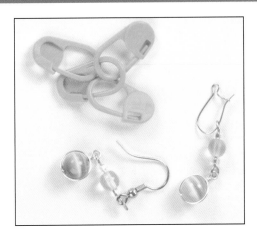

TAPESTRY NEEDLE

A tapestry needle (or yarn needle) has a blunt tip and a large eye to accommodate thick yarns. Use your needle to sew together pieces (see Chapter 6) or to weave in yarn ends after you have completed your project (see Chapter 3).

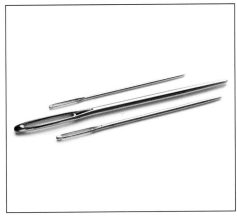

Fiber and construction define a yarn and whether it will be a good match for the project you have in mind. Different types of fibers include natural fibers and synthetic fibers.

NATURAL FIBERS

Natural fibers come from plants or animals. The most common are cotton and wool, but there are many others.

Plant fibers are usually lightweight, can be machine washable, have little stretch, and breathe well. They include cotton, linen, soy, hemp, bamboo, and jute.

Animal fibers are very warm (even when wet), have some natural stretch, and breathe well. They include wool, mohair, cashmere, silk, angora, and alpaca, and generally must be washed by hand, unless they have been treated to be machine-washable (labeled *superwash*).

SYNTHETIC FIBERS

Synthetic fibers are man-made. They include acrylic, nylon, rayon, and polyester. Some synthetics are less expensive than natural fibers, and they tend not to breathe as well. However, as technology advances, synthetic fibers have an increasing number of desirable qualities, including durability, softness, and vibrancy of color.

Note: *Natural and synthetic fibers are often blended so that the resulting yarn benefits from the qualities of each.*

Yarn Construction

Fibers are spun or otherwise constructed into the yarns with which you crochet.

TRADITIONAL YARNS

Traditional yarn is spun by hand or machine and is often plied. Individual strands of spun yarn are called *singles* or a *single ply*. Plying involves taking two or more singles and twisting them together to create a thicker, stronger yarn. Traditional yarns have excellent stitch definition: They show stitches very clearly.

Two-ply yarn consists of two singles twisted together (see photo), and *three-ply* consists of three singles. The twist can be tight or loose; the tightness of the twist helps determine the character of the yarn.

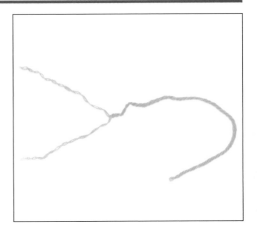

NOVELTY YARNS

Frequently made from synthetic fibers, novelty yarns come in a wide variety of textures and shapes, including eyelash, faux fur, bouclé, ladder, and beaded. Novelty yarns can be used on their own or combined with other yarns to create unique crocheted items.

Note: *Working loosely with a larger hook often makes manipulating a novelty yarn easier. Also, finding stitches made of heavily textured novelty yarns can be confusing. Try working into the spaces between the stitches instead of working into the stitches themselves.*

Each skein or hank of store-bought yarn has a label on which you can find useful information about recommended hook size (see pages 6–9), fiber content (see page 12), care instructions, length, color, and dye lot.

LENGTH

Length is listed in meters (m) or yards (yds.). Use this information to decide how many skeins you need to meet the requirements for a pattern. (See the section "Substitute Different Yarn" on page 18 for more on converting meters and yards.)

Buy yarn according to length, not weight. A 4-ounce skein of lace-weight yarn might contain 1,200 yards, while 4 ounces of bulky-weight yarn might contain just 45 yards.

COLOR NAME/ NUMBER AND DYE LOT

Yarns are dyed in limited quantities, called *dye lots*. Minor variations can occur between lots of the

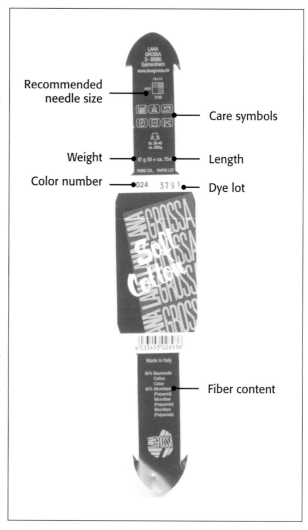

Recommended needle size

Care symbols

Weight

Length

Color number

Dye lot

Fiber content

same color. Yarn manufacturers stamp each label with the code for the dye lot of the yarn, often near where the label lists the color name. When working with multiple skeins of the same color of yarn, make sure that you purchase all skeins from the same dye lot.

CARE SYMBOLS

Although some yarn labels spell out how to wash and dry items made from a particular yarn (see Chapter 6 for more on caring for your crocheted items), universal yarn-care symbols are also frequently used. To avoid accidentally ruining a crocheted item you spent hours creating, refer to the following chart to interpret yarn-care symbols.

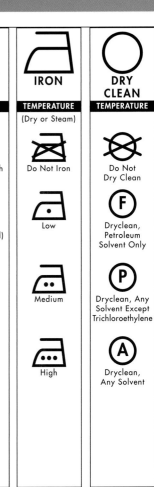

Yarn Weight

STANDARD CATEGORIES

Although we do consider the weight of a ball of yarn, *weight* is also a type of quality a yarn possesses. *Yarn weight* refers to the thickness, or bulkiness, of a strand of yarn. The Craft Yarn Council of America has established the following general, industry-accepted standard categories of yarn weight. Use this chart along with the information on a yarn's label to get an even better idea of how best to use the yarn.

Yarn Weight Symbol	Types of Yarn in Category	Crochet Gauge Range (in SC = 4")	Rec. Hook in Metric	Rec Hook in U.S. Size Range
1 SUPER FINE	Sock, Fingering, Baby	21–32 sts	2.25–3.5 mm	B-1 to E-4
2 FINE	Sport, Baby	16–20 sts	3.5–4.5 mm	E-4 to 7
3 LIGHT	DK, Light Worsted	12–17 sts	4.5–5.5 mm	7 to I-9
4 MEDIUM	Worsted, Afghan, Aran	11–14 sts	5.5–6.5 mm	I-9 to K-10½
5 BULKY	Chunky, Craft, Rug	8–11 sts	6.5–9 mm	K-10½ to M-13
6 SUPER BULKY	Bulky, Roving	5–9 sts	9 mm and larger	M-13 and larger

__Note:__ This chart reflects the most commonly used gauges and needle or hook sizes for specific yarn categories. These are only guidelines. Used with permission of yarnstandards.com

Estimate Yarn Requirements

There is such a large variety of crochet stitches that figuring yardage for a project can be intimidating. The unravel method works well for planning a simple project like a scarf, bag, or blanket.

UNRAVEL METHOD

1 Make a swatch using the yarn and stitch or stitch pattern you have chosen for your project. Note how many rows and stitches fit in an inch. Decide what dimensions your project will have.

   Example: A scarf to measure 5 feet long and 6 inches wide using single crochet. The swatch gauge = 4 stitches in 1 inch and 3 rows in 1 inch. Each row will take 24 stitches; there will be 180 rows.

2 Unravel the number of stitches equal to an inch. Measure the length of the unraveled yarn.

   Example: Unravel 4 stitches = 4 inches of yarn.

3 Multiply this yarn length by the number of inches in the desired finished width of your project. This number is the length of yarn required to make 1 row.

   Example: For a 6-inch-wide scarf: 4 inches of yarn × 6 inches = 24 inches of yarn needed for 1 row.

4 Multiply the number of rows needed by the number of inches of yarn in a row.

   Example: For a 5-foot-long scarf: 180 rows × 24 inches = 4,320 inches.

5 Convert the inches to yards (36 inches = 1 yard). That's how much yarn you need.

   Example: 4,320 inches = 120 yards

TIP

When in doubt, purchase too much yarn. Keep in mind that your gauge may vary slightly throughout a project. Also remember to account for the yarn tails you leave at the beginning and end of your work and every time you change colors or add a new ball of yarn.

Substitute Different Yarn

Crochet patterns specify the yarn that the designer used to create the project. The pattern is based on the gauge she attained. However, you might want to use a different yarn to make the same pattern. The most important thing to do is to use a yarn of the same weight as the one used in the pattern (see the section "Yarn Weight" on page 16). However, even yarns of the same weight can crochet up at a different gauge, and each yarn comes in balls or skeins that might contain a different amount of yarn, so you'll need to do some math to figure out how many balls of the substitute yarn to buy.

Example: Pattern calls for 5 skeins of a worsted-weight yarn; each skein has 114 yds. To substitute a worsted-weight yarn that comes in skeins of 200 yds., do the following:

5 skeins × 114 yds. = 570 yds.

570 yds. ÷ 200 yds. = 2.85

In this scenario, you need 3 skeins of yarn.

Note: *Be sure to keep track of yards and meters—they aren't interchangeable.*
1 meter = 1.1 yards.

TIP

Changing fibers can also affect the outcome of your project. To attain the same effect as the sample in the pattern, it's a good idea to use a yarn with fiber content similar to that of the yarn in the pattern.

How to Handle Store-Bought Yarn

YARN PACKAGING

Store-bought yarn is packaged in one of two ways.

- **Center-pull skein:** The yarn is wound into a ball or cylinder shape. Unwind the yarn from the outside or pull the end out from the inside. Pulling from the inside results in fewer tangles and prevents the skein from rolling around as you pull yarn from it.

- **Hank:** The yarn is wound loosely into a circle and is secured by pieces of string or yarn and then twisted onto itself, creating an attractive, compact skein. You'll need to wind the hank into a ball in order to work with it; otherwise it will tangle almost immediately and become virtually unusable. Handle hanks carefully. Once you remove the ties and start to unwind a hank, it may tangle. Secure the hank before you start to wind the yarn by using one of the following methods:

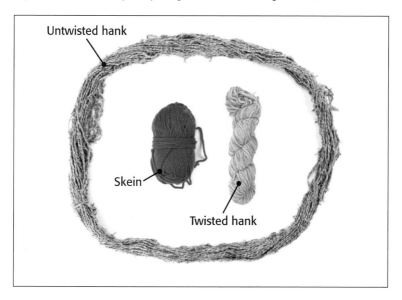

Untwisted hank

Skein

Twisted hank

CONTINUED ON NEXT PAGE

WIND USING A SWIFT

A swift resembles an umbrella; the hank is wrapped around it and the swift spins freely to enable you to wind the yarn easily by hand or with a ball winder.

WIND WITH A CHAIR

1 Wrap the hank around the chair back or,

Turn the chair upside down and use the legs to hold the hank. (Be aware that most chairs will sit at an awkward angle this way, however.)

2 Wind the yarn by hand.

Note: *These methods won't work if you wind the yarn with a ball winder (see "Wind with a Ball Winder"). You'll need to walk around the chair as you wind the yarn by hand.*

WIND WITH A FRIEND

Slip the untwisted hank onto a friend's outstreched forearms. Cut or untie the strings holding the yarn bundled. Starting with an end of yarn, wind it into a ball.

WIND WITH A BALL WINDER

Attach the tail to the ball winder according to the winder's manual. If you're using a swift, wind the yarn, making sure that the swift is spinning freely and the yarn is winding nicely onto the spool. If you're using a friend, use one hand to wind the yarn and the other to help feed the yarn to the winder.

CONTINUED ON NEXT PAGE

WIND A CENTER-PULL SKEIN USING A TOILET-PAPER ROLL

Cut a slit in one end of an empty cardboard toilet-paper roll. Catch the yarn in the slit, leaving a 6-inch tail. Tuck the tail into the tube.

Wind the yarn around the center of the tube in an *x* pattern.

Tuck the end of the yarn through a few layers to secure it. Gently slide the skein off the tube, holding the beginning tail to keep it from getting lost inside the center of the skein. To use the yarn, start with the beginning tail.

TO AVOID TANGLING AFTER WINDING

Some yarns tangle easily regardless of how well wound they are. To help avoid this problem, keep your wound yarn in a plastic sandwich bag, with the yarn fed through a small opening at the top.

TIP

Some yarns, especially some wools, are very delicate and can break easily. Avoid tugging on yarn during winding and after, while you are working with it, to prevent breakage.

You probably already have a growing collection of yarn intended for crochet projects. To prevent current or future frustration, it's important to store and care for your yarn stash properly.

KEEP YARN CLEAN AND DRY

Unused yarn should be stored in a clean dry place to protect it from pests (moths and mice), dirt, and mildew. Although keeping yarn in an airtight bag is a good idea for a limited time, it is important to let natural fibers breathe. Keep wools safe from moths by storing them with cedar chips, lavender sachets, or mothballs, refreshing these moth repellants as needed.

KEEP YARN ORGANIZED

As your yarn collection grows, you will thank yourself for keeping it organized. You may want to organize your yarn by project, by fiber, by weight, or by color. It doesn't matter how you organize it as long as you can easily find the yarn you want! Keep all balls from the same dye lot together so that you know how much you have to work with when a potential project comes up.

The number of storage devices you can use to house your yarn is infinite, but here are a few suggestions:

- Baskets are attractive and can be used as decorations in your home.
- Clear plastic drawers keep your yarn clean and easy to find.
- A bookshelf looks lovely filled with neatly stacked skeins of yarn.

2

Basic Stitches

These stitches and techniques form the basis for almost everything you can do with crochet. See the Crochet Symbols chart on page 46 for the international symbols and abbreviations for some of the basic stitches presented in this chapter.

A slip knot is used to attach the yarn to the hook. Making the knot is the first step in beginning any project.

1 Leaving at least a 6-inch tail, begin to make a simple knot, but do not pull the tail through the loop to complete the knot.

2 Insert your hook under the part of the tail that is within the loop of yarn.

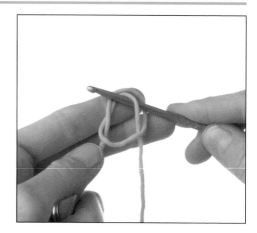

3 Hold the tail and working ends of the yarn and pull gently to tighten the slip knot on the hook.

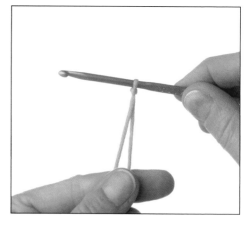

It's not a stitch, and it's not really a technique. But the way you wrap yarn around your hook makes a difference.

Pattern abbreviation: YO or yo

Once you've attached yarn to your hook using a slip knot, you'll create stitches by wrapping yarn around the hook and drawing it through other loops of yarn. The wrapping of the yarn is called making a yarn over, and it consists of wrapping the yarn once around your hook from back to front over the top of the hook.

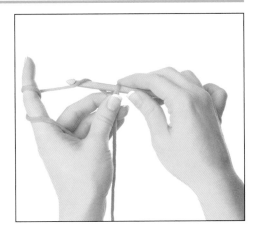

Sometimes yarn overs are made to create extra loops that are not immediately pulled through other loops. Tall stitches like double crochet and treble crochet use yarn overs to create the loops that contribute to their height (see the sections "Double Crochet" and "Treble Crochet").

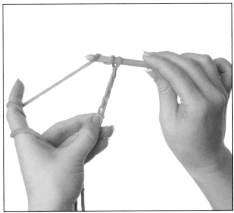

Chain Stitch

The chain stitch is used to create a foundation for most crochet work as well as to create space between other stitches in openwork or lace patterns.

Pattern abbreviation: CH, Ch, ch

---

① Start with a slip knot on the hook. Hold the base of the slip knot and keep your yarn tension with your non-dominant hand.

② Yarn over.

To do a yarn over, wrap the yarn over your hook from back to front so that the yarn is coming toward you over the top of the hook.

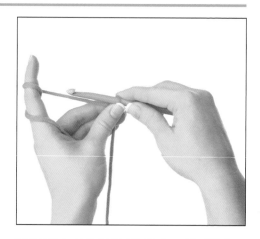

③ Draw the yarn through the loop on your hook (the slip knot).

You've made 1 chain stitch. There is 1 loop left on the hook.

④ Yarn over. Draw the yarn through the loop on the hook.

⑤ Repeat Step 4 until you have made the desired number of chain stitches. (Do not count the slip knot or the loop on the hook as a chain.) Adjust your hold on the chain as it grows so that you're always holding it near the hook.

Keep the chain hanging down from the hook. Don't let the stitches you've made twist around on the hook.

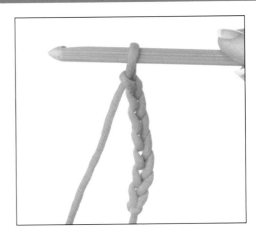

Resist the urge to control your stitches by pulling them tight. If your chain is too tight, it will be very difficult to work stitches into it later. You should have enough room to poke your hook through each chain stitch.

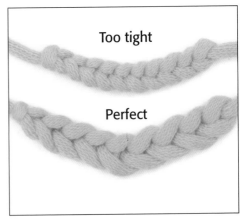

Too tight

Perfect

TIP

Don't be hard on yourself if the process of crocheting the chain feels awkward, or the chain stitches look uneven or twisted. Give yourself 30 minutes or more making chains to get used to the feel of working with the hook and yarn before moving on to another stitch. Soon you'll find your chain looks much better!

To begin a crochet project, you must start with a chain into which you'll work your first row of stitches. Use the chain stitch to create this foundation.

The side facing you as you work the chain stitches looks like a braid or a series of *V*'s.

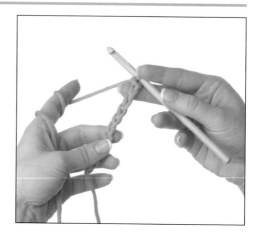

The back of the chain has a ridge down the middle, almost like a spine.

For most patterns and swatches, you work one chain for every stitch you plan to have in the first row (or to account for a lacy pattern that involves skipping stitches), plus additional chains to serve as your first turning chain. Don't count the loop on the hook or the slip knot.

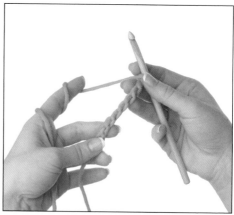

Turning Chains

Crochet stitches can be quite tall. You use chain stitches at the beginning or end of a row to create the height required by the stitches you're making. These *turning chains* keep the edges of your work neat and even.

When you're first starting a project, the number of stitches required for the turning chain is often added to the number needed in the foundation chain. Other times the turning chain instructions are given at the beginning of the first row of the pattern.

Turning chains can be made at the end or beginning of a row. Crochet patterns may specify where to make the chains; if your pattern doesn't, follow your personal preference.

When working in the round, turning chains are required if you join each round, regardless of whether you turn your work before beginning the next round. (They aren't required if you work in a spiral.)

Especially with taller stitches, the turning chain may be counted as a stitch when accounting for the total number of stitches in a row or round. Your pattern will specify if the turning chain is to be counted as a stitch.

Each Stitch Requires a Number of Turning Chains at the Beginning or End of a Row or Round	
Stitch	*Number of Turning Chains*
Slip stitch	0
Single crochet	1
Half double crochet	2
Double crochet	3
Treble crochet	4

Note: See the sections on specific stitches for more information on the number of turning chains required.

This chart is only a guide. With experience, you may find that you prefer to use fewer chains to create a turning chain.

Foundation Single Crochet

This alternative to the basic foundation chain is like working the foundation chain and a row of single crochet all at once. It's stretchy and sturdy, and the same approach can be used for working any of the basic stitches (as for foundation double crochet, etc.).

Pattern abbreviation: Fsc or fsc.

Note: *The foundation single crochet is similar in concept to the extended single crochet stitch (see Chapter 4).*

1. Start with a slip knot on the hook. Chain 2.

2. Insert your hook through both loops of the first chain (the one farthest from your hook). Yarn over and pull up a loop (a).

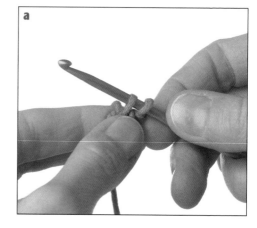

3. Yarn over, draw the yarn through one loop on the hook. This is like making a chain stitch (b).

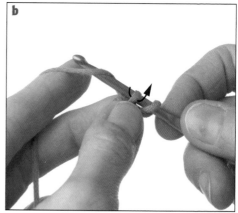

4. Yarn over, draw the yarn through both loops on the hook. One stitch completed (a).

5. Insert your hook through both loops of the chain stitch you made in Step 3. Yarn over and pull up a loop.

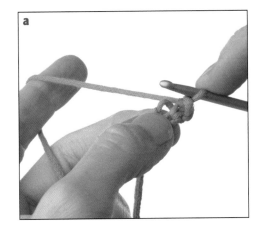

6. Yarn over, draw the yarn through one loop on the hook. Yarn over, draw the yarn through both loops on the hook (b).

Repeat Steps 5 and 6.

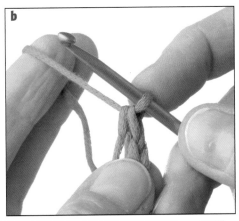

TIP

To substitute foundation stitches for a traditional foundation chain, make one foundation stitch for each stitch called for in the first row of your pattern. You don't need to make extra chains to count as turning chains, since the foundation row also serves as the first row of stitches. To continue with your pattern make a turning chain as directed and proceed to the second row of stitches.

Being familiar with the parts of a chain allows you to subtly alter the look of your work.

When working your first row into the foundation chain, you can insert your hook through one loop of the braid . . .

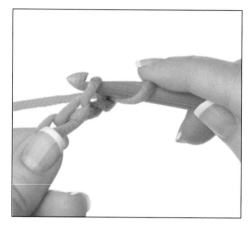

or through both loops of the braid . . .

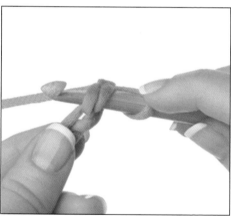

through the ridge loop on the back . . .

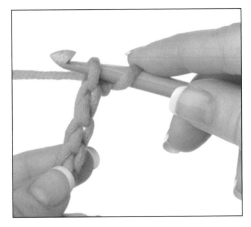

or through the ridge loop along with the top loop of the braid.

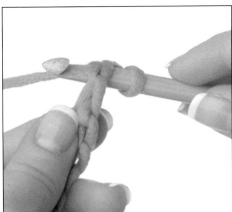

TIP

Working your first row of stitches through the ridge loop only creates a neat foundation edge that will match the final edge of your work.

The slip stitch creates the tightest, shortest, and stiffest of the crochet stitches and is frequently used to stitch squares or panels together when assembling an afghan or other large piece.

• OR ➦

Pattern abbreviation: SL ST, sl st, Sl st, or SS.

Turning chains: 0

① Insert hook into next stitch.

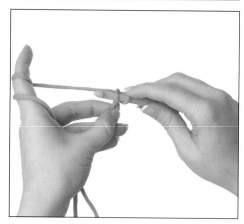

② Yarn over and draw the yarn through the stitch and through loop on hook.

One slip stitch created.

③ Repeat Steps 1 and 2.

Note: Slip stitches are very tight when worked in full rows. Take care to keep your tension loose, or use a hook that is larger than recommended.

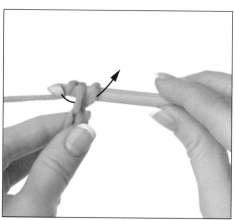

The single crochet stitch is the basic foundation of crochet. Most other stitches are variations on this stitch.

✕ OR ✛

Pattern abbreviation: sc or SC

Turning chains: 1

To begin a project with single crochet, create a foundation chain (see the section "Foundation Chain" on page 32) equal to the number of stitches you require, plus 1. Work your first single crochet into the second chain from your hook.

1 Insert your hook into the next stitch, yarn over, and draw up a loop. There are now two loops on the hook.

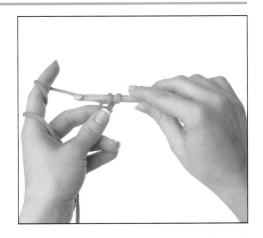

2 Yarn over and draw the yarn through both loops on the hook.

There is now one loop on the hook. One single crochet created.

3 Repeat Steps 1–2.

Half Double Crochet

Half double crochet is a versatile stitch that is commonly used to make garments, hats, and other accessories.

Pattern abbreviation: hdc or HDC

Turning chains: 2

When working into a foundation chain, work your first half double crochet into the third chain from your hook.

1 Yarn over once, insert your hook into the next stitch, yarn over, and draw up a loop. There are now three loops on the hook.

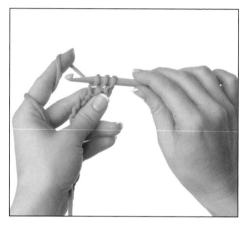

2 Yarn over and draw the yarn through all three loops on the hook.

One loop remains on the hook. One half-double crochet created.

3 Repeat Steps 1–3.

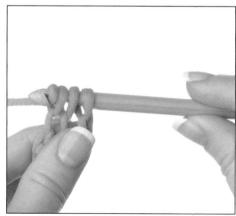

Like half double crochet, you make a double crochet stitch by doing a yarn over before inserting your hook into the next stitch.

Pattern abbreviation: DC or dc

Turning chains: 3

When working into a foundation chain, work your first double crochet into the fourth chain from your hook.

① Yarn over once, insert your hook into the next stitch, yarn over, and draw up a loop. There are now three loops on the hook.

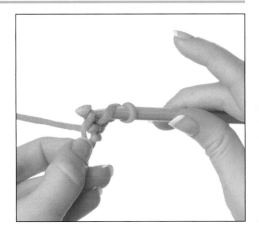

② Yarn over and draw the yarn through the first two loops on the hook.

There are now two loops on the hook.

CONTINUED ON NEXT PAGE

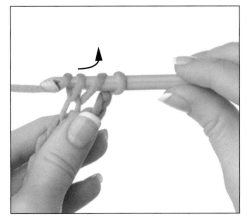

③ Yarn over and draw the yarn through the two remaining loops on the hook.

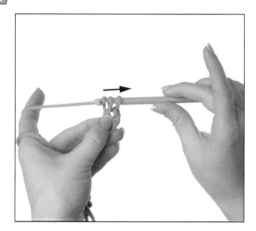

One double crochet created.

④ Repeat Steps 1–3.

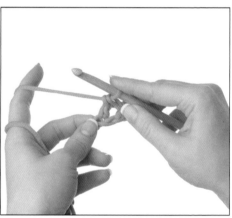

TIP

Because the turning chain may count as a double crochet, work into it as though it is a double crochet unless your pattern tells you otherwise. To do so, insert your hook into the top (third) chain of the turning chain.

Treble crochet (triple crochet) is a very tall stitch created by making two yarn overs before inserting your hook into the next stitch. This fabric has more drape than fabric made from some other stitches.

Pattern abbreviation: tr or TR

Turning chains: 4

When working into a foundation chain, work your first treble crochet into the fifth chain from your hook.

1 Yarn over twice, insert your hook into the next stitch, yarn over, and draw up a loop. There are now four loops on the hook.

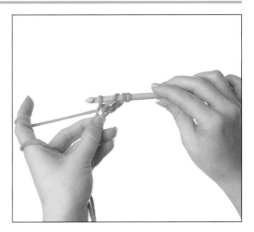

2 Yarn over and draw the yarn through the first two loops on the hook. There are now three loops on the hook.

3 Yarn over and draw the yarn through the next two loops on the hook. There are now two loops on the hook.

CONTINUED ON NEXT PAGE

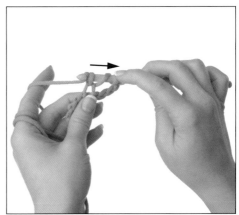

④ Yarn over and draw the yarn through both loops on the hook.

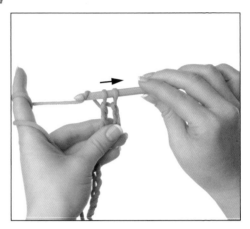

One treble crochet created.

⑤ Repeat Steps 1–5.

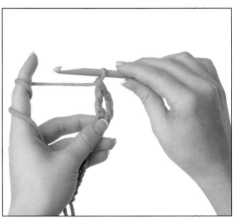

TIP

Because the turning chain may count as a treble crochet, work into it as though it is a treble crochet unless your pattern tells you otherwise. To do so, insert your hook into the top (fourth) chain of the turning chain.

Count Your Stitches

You need to count the number of stitches in each row or round of your work to determine whether you're achieving the correct gauge for the pattern you've chosen. Keeping track of how many stitches are in a working piece is also important—often, counting stitches is the best way to diagnose mistakes.

There are two easy ways to identify an individual stitch in your work:

- Examine the tops of the stitches. The top of each crochet stitch looks like a braid or a *V*. Each braid or *V* corresponds to one stitch.

- Examine the post of the stitch. The post is the body of the stitch. Just count the posts to see how many stitches you have made.

Some patterns—especially those published in Europe and Asia—utilize stitch symbols to convey crochet instructions. Use this chart to determine what each symbol represents.

chain stitch (**ch**)	◯	V-stitch (**V-st**)	
slip stitch (**sl st**)	• OR ➡	crossed double crochet (**crossed dc**)	OR
single crochet (**sc**)	✕ OR +	shell [of 4 dc]	
half double crochet (**hdc**)		picot [of ch 3, sl st]	
double crochet (**dc**)		cluster [of 4 dc]	
treble crochet (**tr**)		reverse [sc]	
double treble crochet (**dtr**)		puff st [of 3 dc]	
triple treble crochet (**trtr**)		popcorn (**pop** or **pc**) [of 5 dc]	
single crochet in front loop only (**fb**)	**X**	bobble [composed of 5 loops]	
single crochet in back loop only (**bb**)	✕	loop stitch (**loop st**)	
front post double crochet (**FP dc**)		long stitch (**long st**) or spike	
back post double crochet (**BP dc**)			

Crochet is a fun skill to share with a child. The chain stitch alone can keep one enthralled for hours. Whether a child wishes to learn every stitch possible or simply wants to make a mile-long chain, you're likely to find your time together with crochet inspiring!

TO START

Handling a crochet hook and yarn can be tricky for very small hands.

Place the slip knot on the hook and show the child how you hold the yarn and hook. With both your hands and her hands on the yarn and hook, steer her through the motions of making a chain stitch, talking through what you are doing to make the stitch.

Allow the child to work the stitches without your help. If handling the yarn and hook in separate hands is too difficult, try this super simple method: Hold the hook in the hook hand, yarn over with the yarn hand, drop the yarn, using the yarn hand pull the loop on the hook over the yarn over and off the hook. It can be hard to work single crochet and other stitches this way, but it will get anyone moving on a chain.

JAZZ UP THAT CROCHET CHAIN!

Add fun beads to the yarn before you start crocheting. Slide a bead up with the yarn over and work it into a chain stitch. This is a great way for a child to make bracelets to share with friends.

You can also combine different colors or a smooth yarn with something fuzzy and crochet the two yarns using a jumbo hook.

TIP

Sitting close together, have her "help" you with your own work. Hold the hook and yarn together by steering the small hands through the work.

chapter 3

Basic Techniques

Shaping, working in the round, changing colors, and finishing off a project are essential skills. Brush up on them and you'll stitch your project smoothly from start to finish.

See the Crochet Symbols chart in Chapter 2 (page 46) for the international symbols and abbreviations for some of the techniques presented in this chapter.

Use increases to add one or more stitches to a round or row.

Pattern abbreviation: INC or inc

AT THE BEGINNING OR END OF A ROW

Make chains to add one or more stitches to the beginning of the next row. This is a dramatic increase.

Note: *This technique is only used when working in rows, not in rounds.*

1. At the end of the row, work a chain stitch for each increased stitch, plus the turning chain (see Chapter 2 for more about turning chains).

2. Turn your work. Skip the number of chains required for the turning chain. Work stitches into the top loops of the extra chains.

3. Continue the row as directed.

   Note: *Count your stitches at the end of an increase row to make sure you have the correct number.*

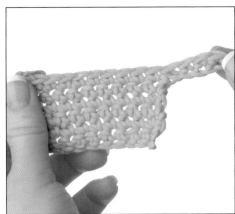

WITHIN A ROW OR ROUND

Work two or more stitches into one stitch to create an increase within a row or round.

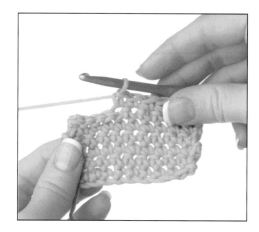

① Work a stitch as directed.

② Work the next stitch by inserting your hook into the same stitch as in Step 1.

TIP

To increase by three stitches at once, work four stitches into a single stitch from the previous row, or spread the increases over multiple stitches for more subtlety.

Use decreases to reduce the number of stitches in a row or round. There are several methods for decreasing; those covered in this section are indicated without special symbols.

Pattern abbreviation: DEC or dec

SKIP A STITCH

Skip the next stitch and work into the stitch after it as usual. This method leaves a small hole in the fabric where the stitch was skipped. Some patterns use this method to create decorative holes in the fabric.

LEAVE STITCHES UNWORKED AT THE BEGINNING OF A ROW

Do not make a turning chain but do turn your work. Work a slip stitch (see Chapter 2) into each of the stitches from the previous row to be decreased (a). Make a turning chain necessary for the height of the row but don't turn. Continue with the row as usual. This creates a sharp decrease on one side. On the next row, do not work into the slip stitches (b).

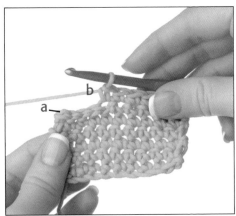

LEAVE STITCHES UNWORKED AT THE END OF A ROW

At the end of a row, do not work the final stitches equal to the number to be decreased. Leaving these stitches unworked, make a turning chain, turn, and proceed with the next row as directed.

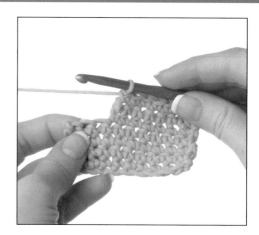

TIP

Leaving stitches unworked creates dramatic shaping and is often used in garment construction. This type of decrease, for obvious reasons, cannot be used when working in the round. To create subtle shaping, see the next section, "Decrease by Working Stitches Together."

Use this flexible decrease method at any point in a row or round.

Pattern abbreviation: st#TOG (with "st" replaced by the stitch to be used and "#" replaced by the number of stitches to be worked together, as in dc2TOG). Any number of stitches can be worked together, depending on the desired shaping effect.

Note: This type of decrease can be used with any basic stitch. Double crochet is used as an example here.

1 Work the double crochet stitch as usual until the final step, when two loops remain on the hook. Do not complete the stitch.

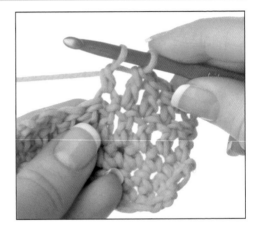

2 Yarn over, insert the hook into the next stitch and work to the same point. There are now three loops on the hook. Yarn over and draw the yarn through all three loops.

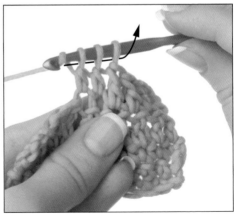

3 The decrease looks like two stitches sharing a single top.

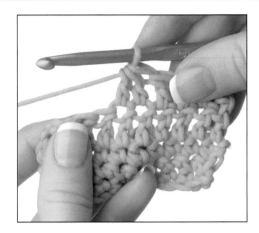

For gradual shaping, use one or more 2TOGs worked over the course of a row or round. For a sharper decrease, use 3TOG or 4TOG by repeating Step 2 until four or five loops remain on the hook, respectively.

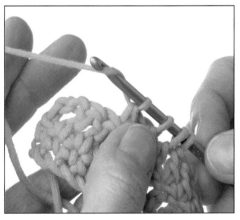

IN A TUBE

Although not as common a practice as crocheting in the round from the center out (see next section), it's simple to crochet a tube. Legwarmers are a great example of a crocheted tube!

1. Make a chain as directed, slip stitch in the first chain to form a ring.

2. Work the first round of stitches into the individual chains or around the chain, depending on your pattern or your preference.

   Note: Unlike when you crochet from the center out, it is not necessary that you shape your work when you crochet in a tube, unless you want the diameter of the tube to change.

3. If you choose to work in rounds (see opposite page) join the last stitch of the round to the first stitch of the round with a slip stitch, create a turning chain and work the next round. If you choose to work without joining rounds (see spiral method on opposite page) simply continue to work stitch into each stitch from the previous round.

WORK FROM THE CENTER

When beginning in the center of the round, increasing is used to shape the piece as it grows (see the "Increasing" section of this chapter). Hats, baskets, toys, and bags are often made from the center out. There are several ways to begin crocheting in the round from the center, which we cover after the next section on joining rounds (see "Join Rounds").

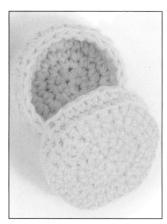

JOIN ROUNDS

To work your piece in concentric circles, use a slip stitch to join the last stitch of the round to the first, and then make a turning chain before starting the next round. (It is common not to turn to work the next round in the opposite direction; regardless, the chain is called a turning chain.)

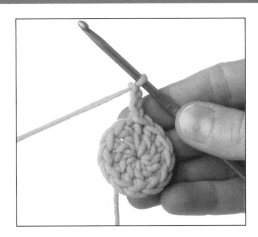

WORK IN A SPIRAL

To work your piece without joining each round, simply keep crocheting. Use a stitch marker to indicate the first or last stitch of the round so you don't lose your place; remove the marker to work the stitch and immediately place the marker in the stitch you just made.

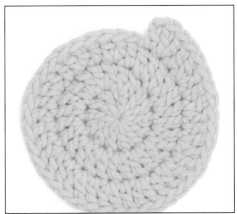

TIP

Note that the final stitch of a spiral is not flush with the first stitch of its round. To even this out slightly, end with a shorter stitch in the next stitch before you fasten off.

You can use the chain stitch to create a ring as a foundation for working in the round. This method creates a strong center and will likely leave a hole in the center of your piece.

1 Chain five.

Note: We're using five chains as an example. This technique can be used with any number of chains greater than three.

2 Slip stitch (see Chapter 2) in the fifth chain from the hook (the first chain you made).

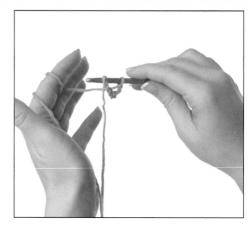

There are different ways to work into the ring:

1 Work into each chain stitch as you would work into a foundation chain.

2 Ignore the individual chain stitches and work around the chain, through the center of the ring. To do this, insert your hook through the center of the ring, yarn over, and draw the yarn around the chains. Complete the stitch as usual.

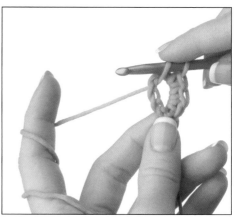

Using a loop to form your foundation for working in the round creates an invisible, adjustable ring. The first round of stitches is worked into the loop.

① Begin with a slip knot on your hook, leaving a longer tail than usual.

② Wrap the yarn tail twice around your two middle fingers to create a loop.

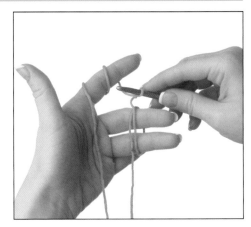

③ Insert your hook into the ring. Yarn over.

④ Draw the yarn through, and continue to draw it through the loop on the hook (the slip knot; see photo). One slip stitch made.

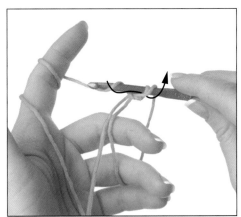

CONTINUED ON NEXT PAGE

5 Work the appropriate number of chains to create the turning chain for the stitch you're using. Proceed by making the required number of stitches into the ring.

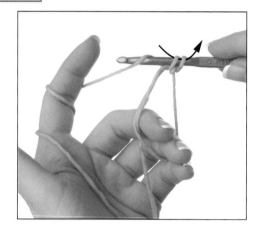

6 Pull the yarn tail gently but firmly to tighten and close the ring.

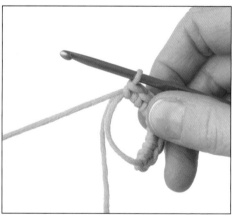

TIP

This ring may loosen with wear and tear. It's important to weave in the tail from the loop and anchor it securely inside the stitches.

This method for starting to work in the round is more flexible than using many chain stitches, and it's less flexible than using a loop.

1 Start with a slip knot on your hook. Chain two.

2 Work all single crochet stitches of your first round into the second chain from your hook (a).

Note: If you're working in half double crochet, double crochet, or treble crochet, start with three, four, or five chains, respectively, and work all stitches into the chain that is farthest from your hook.

The chain stitch will expand to accommodate a large number of stitches.

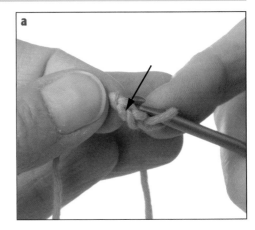

Pull the tail gently to tighten the chain stitch (b). Working your stitches into the back loop of the chain allows you to pull the yarn tail to tighten the center of the ring after you've completed the first round of stitches. (See Chapter 4 for more on working into the back loop only.)

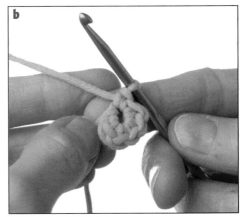

Working in the round from the center out often involves creating a flat circle. In order to accomplish this, increases are made evenly throughout each round. This table displays the distribution of increases for several common stitch counts.

Gradual, Spaced Increases				
Round 1:	5 stitches	6 stitches	7 stitches	8 stitches
Round 2: Increase in every stitch for a total of:	10 stitches	12 stitches	14 stitches	16 stitches
Round 3: Increase in every other stitch for a total of:	15 stitches	18 stitches	21 stitches	24 stitches
Round 4: Increase in every third stitch for a total of:	20 stitches	24 stitches	28 stitches	32 stitches
Round 5: Increase in every fourth stitch for a total of:	25 stitches	30 stitches	35 stitches	40 stitches
Round 6: Increase in every fifth stitch for a total of:	30 stitches	36 stitches	42 stitches	48 stitches
Round 7: Increase in every sixth stitch for a total of:	35 stitches	42 stitches	49 stitches	56 stitches
Round 8: Increase in every seventh stitch for a total of:	40 stitches	48 stitches	56 stitches	64 stitches

TIP

Notice that each round contains a number of evenly spaced increases equal to the number of stitches in Round 1. Distributing the increases as directed creates a polygon instead of a true circle (this is especially noticeable when you have worked several rounds). To create a true circle, work the same number of increases in each round but stagger where you place the first one so that you're not placing the increases in the same place on each round.

Whether it's time to switch to a new ball of yarn because you're running out or because you simply want to change to a different color or texture, you can make the switch at any point in your work.

① Work the final stitch with the original yarn until only two loops remain on the hook. Do not complete the stitch.

② Yarn over with the original yarn and the new yarn held together. Leave a 6-inch tail of new yarn hanging off the back of the hook.

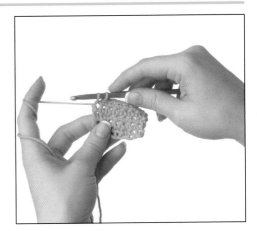

③ Draw both yarns through the loops on the hook to complete the stitch.

Note: *See Chapter 5 for more on working with different colors of yarn.*

CONTINUED ON NEXT PAGE

④ Drop the old yarn. Continue crocheting as directed with the new yarn, only. If you've changed yarn at the end of a row, make your turning chain and turn.

⑤ If you have changed yarn in the middle of a row, continue to work across the row as normal.

Note: *You'll need to weave in the tails left by the old and new yarns (see "Weave In Yarn Ends").*

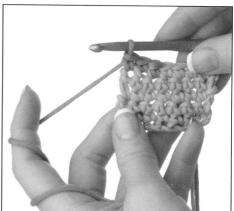

TIP

This stitch where two yarns are combined may be a bit fragile, which makes weaving in the ends important. Weave in the ends securely and the stitch will stay put.

Fasten Off

To secure your yarn so that your stitches don't unravel when you've completed your project, you need to fasten off.

---

1. Complete the final stitch. Cut the yarn, leaving a tail at least 6 inches long.
2. Yarn over and draw the entire tail through the loop. Pull tight.

TIP

When you put a crochet project down for a while you may wish to temporarily fasten off. Simply make a loop large enough to pull your entire ball of yarn through. If the little knot isn't too tight you can loosen the loop and pull your yarn back through when you're ready to crochet again.

Every project involves at least two yarn tails: one created when you made your slip knot or beginning loop, and one left when you fasten off. You also leave yarn tails when you add new yarn or change colors. Weave the tails into your work to avoid unsightly, bumpy knots and to prevent your stitches from unraveling.

Use a tapestry needle to weave yarn tails through the stitches on the *wrong side* of the fabric to secure them and hide them from view. The wrong side is the side that will not face out when the piece is completed (on a garment, the side worn against the skin).

To make sure the tail remains secure, create a U, C, or Z shape as you sew the yarn into the crochet stitches. The more zigzags there are, the less likely the yarn will come out.

When you're sure you've woven in enough that the tail won't slip out, tug on the crochet fabric in all directions to settle the tail in place. Cut the end of the tail if necessary.

Advanced Stitches

Building on the basics opens up infinite possibilities for texture, structure, lace, and beyond.

Slight variations in how you make your stitches can create subtle differences in the look and feel of your crocheted fabric. Stitch combinations like popcorns and bobbles can add playful textures, while the knot stitches work up to make a quick lacy fabric.

The double treble crochet stitch (also known as quadruple crochet) is a very tall stitch.

Pattern abbreviation: DTR or dtr

Turning chains: 5

When working into a foundation chain: Work your first DTR into the sixth chain from your hook.

① YO three times, insert the hook into the next stitch, YO, and pull up a loop. There are now five loops on the hook.

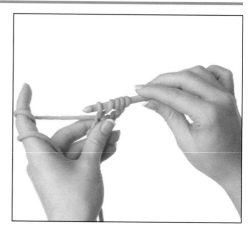

② YO and draw the yarn through the first two loops on the hook. There are now four loops on the hook.

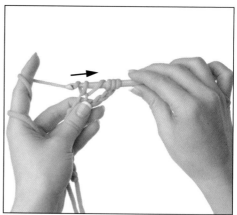

③ YO and draw the yarn through the next two loops on the hook. There are now three loops on the hook.

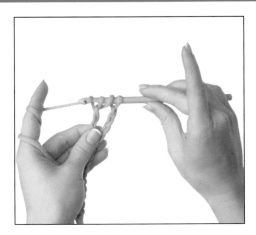

④ YO and draw the yarn through the next two loops on the hook. There are now two loops on the hook.

⑤ YO and draw the yarn through both loops on the hook. You have created one double treble crochet.

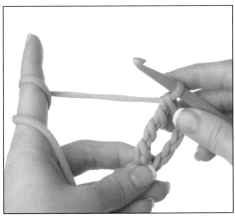

TIP

Because the turning chain likely counts as a double treble crochet in your pattern, work into the top chain of it as though it were a proper stitch, unless your pattern tells you otherwise.

Some patterns call for even taller stitches. Triple treble starts with four yarn overs and follows the same progression of steps: Continue to work the stitch as you would the double treble, until one loop remains on the hook.

Extended Crochet Stitches

Extended crochet stitches are a family of stitches, each a half step taller than the corresponding basic stitch.

Pattern abbreviation: Extended stitches are indicated with an 'E' (e.g., Esc, Edc, and so on)

Turning chains: Extended stitches require one more turning chain than the basic stitch.

EXTENDED SINGLE CROCHET

When working into a foundation chain: Work your first extended single crochet into the third chain from your hook.

1. Insert the hook into the next stitch, YO, and draw up a loop. There are now two loops on the hook.

2. YO and draw the yarn through the first loop on the hook. There are now two loops on the hook.

   Note: Add Step 2 to any basic stitch to make an extended crochet stitch.

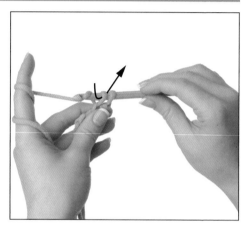

3. YO and draw the yarn through both loops on the hook. You have created one extended single crochet.

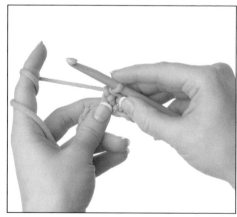

Working into only one loop instead of both loops of a stitch is the simplest way to change the texture and drape of your crochet. Patterns indicate whether to work into the front loop or back loop only; if no mention is made, work into both loops.

Pattern abbreviations: Front Loop Only: flo, FLO; Back Loop Only: blo, BLO

Turning chains: as usual

FRONT LOOP

The front loop is the loop closest to you when you're holding your crochet work in front of you.

Note: *The FLO symbol is in bold-face at the top of this page.*

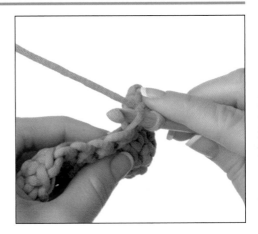

BACK LOOP

The back loop is the one farthest from you.

Note: *The BLO symbol is in light-face at the top of this page.*

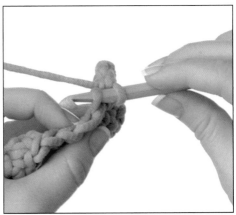

CONTINUED ON NEXT PAGE

Work in Front Loop or Back Loop Only *(continued)*

WHEN TO USE FLO OR BLO

After working a few rows using both loops, crochet an entire row working into the front loop only (see photo). The unworked loops create a little ridge on one side of the fabric. Working into the back loop only will create a ridge on the other side of the fabric. This subtle touch makes a nice border on the edge of a simple hat.

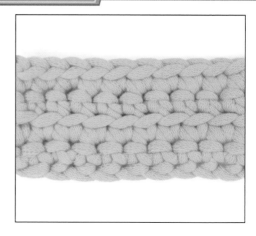

Working into only one loop for an entire piece creates a fabric with gentle drape and more give. Working into the back loop only, specifically, creates a ribbing effect. The fabric feels less dense than when both loops are worked. To create a rumpled texture, alternate between working stitches into the front and back loops of the same row.

TIP

Working into the front loop is sometimes referred to as front porch stitch. Likewise, working into the back loop is sometimes called back porch stitch.

You can use spike stitches to add elaborate-looking details to crocheted fabric. Just work into any space below the top loops of the stitches from the previous row, resulting in a "spike" of yarn connecting the stitch to the current working row.

① Instead of inserting your hook into the top loops of the next stitch, insert your hook into the space directly below the next stitch from the previous row.

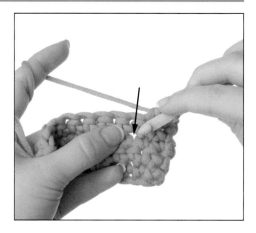

② YO and draw up a loop. Pull this loop up to the working row, taking care not to pull the stitch too tight.

③ YO and draw the yarn through both loops on the hook.

You have created one single crochet spike stitch (see photo).

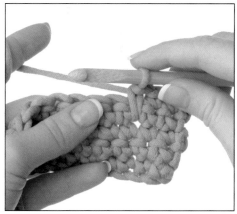

CONTINUED ON NEXT PAGE

WORK ALTERNATING SINGLE CROCHETS AND SPIKES

Alternate single crochets and spikes in the same row. This effect is striking as a border.

WORK LONG SPIKES

Make longer spikes by working into a space several rows below the working row. When drawing up a loop, be sure to make it nice and long. Doing so prevents the fabric from buckling.

Combine single crochets with long spikes to add dramatic detail.

Work *1 SC, 1 long spike. Repeat from * to end of row.

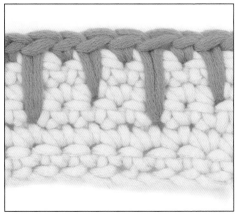

TIP

Spike stitches can be used in a variety of ways to add interest to your crochet work. Any of the above simple combinations can be used as a border or within a piece.

Working around the post of the stitch from the previous row creates stitches in relief, often to create ribs or cables.

Pattern abbreviations: Front Post Double Crochet: FPdc or FPDC; Back Post Double Crochet; BPdc or BPDC

Turning chains: usual # − 1

FRONT POST DOUBLE CROCHET

Post stitches cannot be worked into the foundation chain; you must begin with a foundation row of tall stitches (for instance double crochet, as in this example).

Note: *Because a post stitch is shorter than a stitch worked into the top of another stitch, the turning chain for a post stitch is shorter by one chain.*

1 YO. Insert the hook from front to back to front around the post of the stitch in the previous row.

2 YO and draw the yarn around the post to pull up a loop. Complete the double crochet.

CONTINUED ON NEXT PAGE

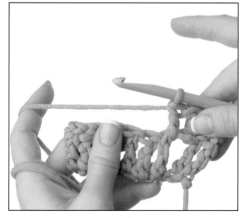

BACK POST DOUBLE CROCHET

For this example, start with a row of double crochet. At the end of this foundation row, chain two for the turning chain and turn.

① YO. Insert the hook from back to front to back around the post of the stitch in the previous row.

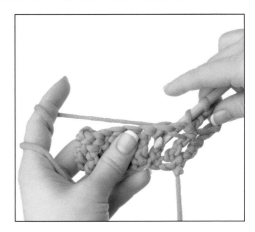

② YO and draw up a loop. Complete the double crochet.

Note: We use double crochet as an example here; treble crochet post stitches are worked in the same manner.

Note: There is also Front Post Treble Crochet (FPtc or FPTC) and Back Post Treble Crochet (BPtc or BPTC).

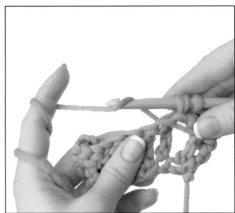

TIP

To create ribbing, use an even number of stitches. Begin by working a FPDC into the first stitch and a BPDC into the next stitch. Continue alternating FPDCs and BPDCs across the row. Make a turning chain and turn. Repeat this row to create a ribbed pattern.

Clusters

Clusters are in a category that includes a variety of stitch combinations, such as those worked together to create bobbles, and puffs. The stitches in a basic cluster are joined at the top similar to decreases, and can be worked into one space or over several spaces. See Chapter 3 for more on how to work stitches together to decrease.

Pattern abbreviation: CL or cl

Note: This example uses treble crochet (see Chapter 2), but clusters can be made in any stitch.

1 Work a treble crochet until the final step, when two loops remain on the hook. Do not complete the stitch.

2 Insert the hook into the next stitch and work another treble crochet to the same point. There are now three loops on the hook.

3 Repeat Step 2 to create a partial treble crochet in the next stitch. There are now three partial treble crochets (four loops on the hook).

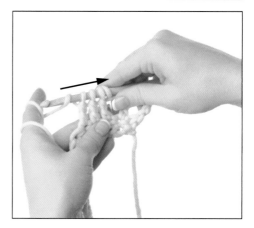

4 YO and draw the yarn through all four loops.

Note: The only difference between the cluster in this example and a tr3tog decrease is the intent. Clusters are usually used to create an interesting stitch pattern; decreases are used to shape the work.

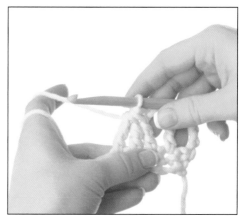

Bobbles

A cluster of tall stitches is worked into the same space and joined together at the top, creating a bobble that stands out.

Pattern abbreviation: BO or bo

1 Work a double crochet as usual until the final step, when two loops remain on the hook. Do not complete the stitch.

2 Insert the hook back into the same stitch and work another double crochet to the same point. There are now three loops on the hook.

3 Repeat Step 2 to create two more partial double crochet stitches. There are now four partial double crochets; five loops on the hook (see photo).

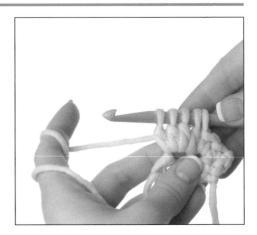

4 YO and draw the yarn through all five loops.

5 CH 1. You have made one bobble.

Note: When working into the top of bobbles, it looks like there are two stitches to work into. Skip the chain from the top of the bobble and work into the stitch.

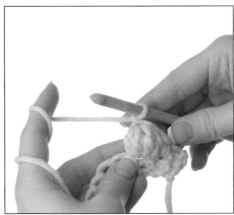

Puffs

Puff stitches are bobbles worked with a half-double crochet (see Chapter 2) instead of a taller stitch. This results in the puff being shorter and puffier than a bobble.

Pattern abbreviation: PS or ps

1 YO. Insert the hook into the next stitch, YO, and draw a loop through the stitch. This loop should be looser than the loop normally created when working a half double crochet.

2 Repeat Step 1 in the same stitch three more times (four partial half double crochets in total).

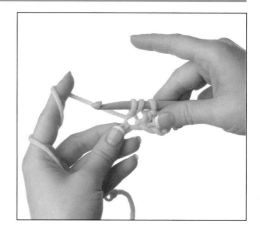

There are now nine loops on the hook (see photo). YO and draw the yarn through all nine loops.

3 CH 1 to complete the stitch. You have created one puff stitch.

Note: *When working from a pattern with a symbol chart, the symbol for a given cluster, bobble, puff, or popcorn will reflect the type and number of stitches used in that specific pattern.*

A popcorn consists of several tall stitches worked into the same space. Unlike a bobble, each stitch in a popcorn is worked to completion, and then all are gathered together in the final step.

Pattern abbreviation: PC or pc

① Work four double-crochet stitches into the next stitch.

② Slip your hook out of the remaining loop (see photo).

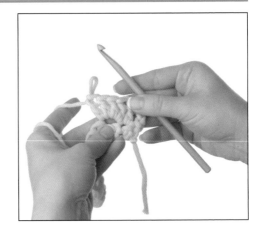

③ Insert your hook into the top of the first double-crochet from this group and then back into the empty loop. Draw the loop through the top of that stitch and CH one to finish the popcorn.

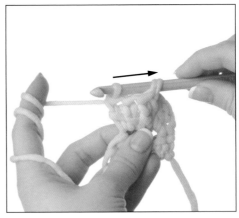

Bullions

The bullion stitch breaks from the standard format of most crochet stitches. This stitch involves making many yarn overs (from six to ten, depending on the pattern) and has a texture all its own. When making a bullion, keep the yarn overs loose. You can use your fingers to ease your hook through the loops one by one.

Pattern abbreviation: BS or bs

---

① YO eight times. Insert the hook in the next stitch, YO, and draw up a loop.

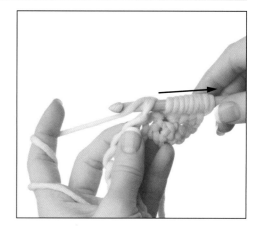

② YO and draw the yarn over through all the loops on the hook.

③ YO and draw the yarn through the remaining loop on the hook. You have completed one bullion stitch.

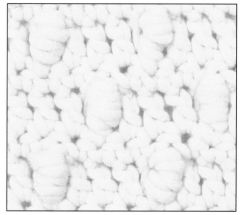

You work a Clones knot over the three chains closest to the hook.

① CH 3. YO and wrap the yarn around the CH-3 as follows: Swing the hook from the front, under the chain, to the back (see photo).

② YO and swing back under the chain to the front.

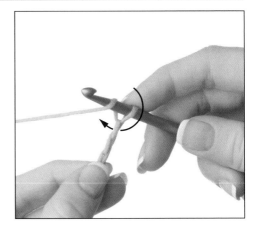

③ Repeat Step 1 four more times. There are now 11 loops on the hook.

Note: *As you work the yarn overs, you are working over and covering three chains. If you have covered more than that, simply push the loops together.*

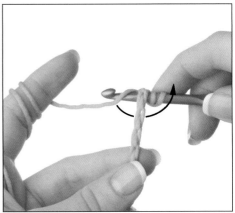

4 YO and draw the yarn through all 11 loops.

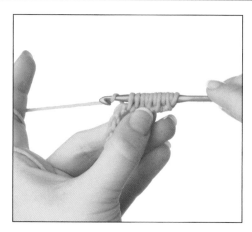

5 Sl st into the third chain to complete the Clones knot.

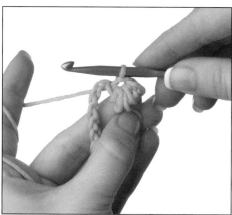

TIP

To add a Clones knot to an edging similar to the picot edging on page 148, do the following: Work 1 SC into the next stitch, * CH 6, work the clones knot over the first 3 stitches from the hook, CH 3, skip a few stitches and work 1 SC in the next stitch. Repeat from * across.

Also known as a Solomon's knot, this stitch is made by drawing up a long loop and then locking it with a stitch at the top of the loop.

① CH 1 and lengthen the loop on the hook.

Note: *It is important that the length of each loop is the same so that the stitches match. A good way to keep track is to compare the loop to a given part of your finger. Knuckles make great guideposts. Here, the loop is being measured to the second knuckle.*

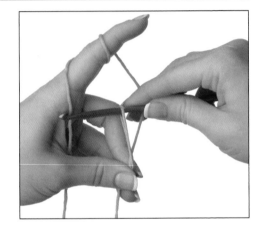

② YO and draw the yarn through the long loop.

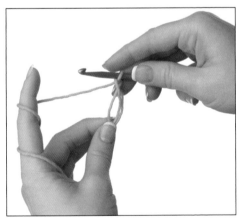

3 Insert your hook between the long loop and the strand from the yarn over. YO and draw the yarn through this space.

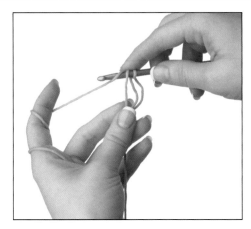

4 YO and draw the yarn through both loops remaining on the hook.

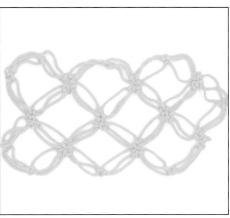

TIP

The Lover's knot can be used to make a lacy fabric of knots; it's also a quick and fun way to make accessories. Make a funky scarf combining several lengths of Lover's knots, or slip beads into the action with the YO in Step 2.

chapter **5**

Beyond the Basic Techniques

Sometimes crochet involves manipulating basic stitches in iconic ways (as with granny squares or tapestry crochet) or taking a whole new approach to the craft (as with Tunisian crochet or hairpin lace). This chapter covers several techniques that open up a whole new world of craft.

Felting/ Fulling

Untreated wool and other animal fibers mat and shrink when agitated. This results in a fuzzy, dense fabric that is strong and extremely durable. Dive in and have fun!

Felting refers to the process of agitating raw fibers until they bind together; *fulling* refers to agitating stitched fibers (including knitted or crocheted fibers) until they bind together. Although fulling is technically the correct term for doing this with crochet, the term *felting* has become the popular way to refer to all methods that deal with agitating and matting wool.

FELT TEST SWATCHES FIRST

Before crocheting an entire project for fulling, felt some swatches using the yarn and stitch you plan to use so you can determine how severely the fabric felts and how much it shrinks lengthwise and widthwise. If you are following a pattern, this is the same as working a gauge swatch. You can compare your results to the dimensions specified in the pattern and make adjustments if needed. If you aren't working with a pattern, use the swatches to plan your project.

To crochet fabric for felting, use a larger hook than usual so that the fibers have room to agitate and bind together.

You might want to experiment with hook size and with which stitch you use, as different stitches produce different felted fabrics.

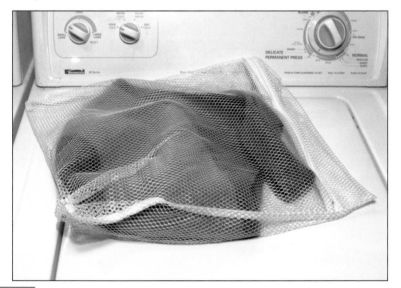

FELT A CROCHETED ITEM

1. To keep the fabric from getting pulled out of shape, place it into a mesh bag, zippered laundry bag, or pillowcase.

2. Set your washing machine to a warm or hot wash and add a small amount of mild soap or detergent. Place the mesh bag and one or two pairs of jeans into the machine. The jeans help with agitation.

3. Once the agitation cycle starts, check on your piece every five minutes until it is the desired size and texture.

Note: *You may have to run the washing machine through several agitation cycles for adequate fulling. Avoid the spin cycle; it may stretch and warp the piece.*

4. When you've finished felting your piece, rinse it gently. Without wringing, wrap it in a towel or two, and press to remove any excess water.

5. Block your piece. If you're blocking a 3-D item such as a bag or a hat, fill it with rolled towels or plastic bags until it's the proper shape. Let it dry. Drying may take a day or two.

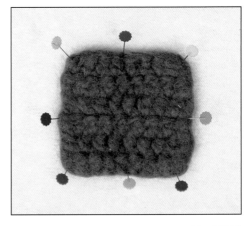

TIP

Read yarn labels carefully to make sure your yarn is suited for felting or fulling. Wool that has been treated to make it machine washable (marked "superwash") will not felt or full when agitated.

Bleaches, dyes, and blending other fibers with the wool can affect a yarn's reaction to agitation. Some won't felt or full, others might felt only a little.

Tunisian crochet involves making each row in two steps by using a long Tunisian (or Afghan) hook. First, you pick up all the stitches (Forward Pass), and then you bind them off (Return Pass). To get started, make a Foundation Forward Pass.

Pattern abbreviation: Tss (Tunisian Simple Stitch).

TUNISIAN SIMPLE STITCH

Foundation Forward Pass

The foundation row is the same for any variation of Tunisian crochet.

1. Make a chain equal to the number of stitches you require.

2. Insert your hook into the second chain. YO and draw up a loop.

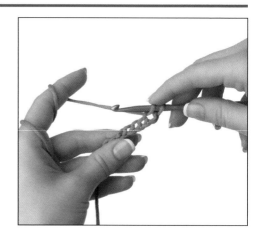

3. Insert the hook into the next chain, YO and draw up a loop.

4. Repeat Step 3 until you reach the end of the row. Do not turn your work.

   You now have one loop on your hook for each chain.

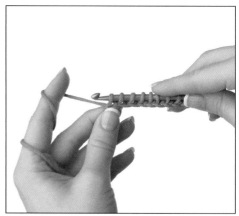

Foundation Return Pass

In a return pass, you essentially bind off each stitch that you picked up in the forward pass. You work the foundation return pass with the right side of the work facing you. Do not turn the work.

1. YO and draw the yarn through one loop on the hook.

2. YO and draw the yarn through two loops on the hook.

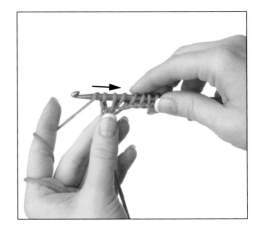

3. Repeat Step 2 until you reach the end of the return row. YO and draw through the final two stitches. At the end of the row, one loop remains on the hook.

CONTINUED ON NEXT PAGE

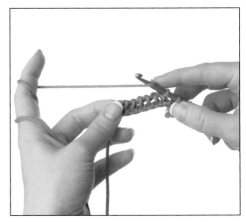

TIP

If your Tunisian crochet curls, try moving up a hook size to loosen up the fabric. Tunisian crochet is known for its dense, rich texture, but did you know that when worked with a much larger hook the same stitches take on a fantastic lacy drape?

TSS Forward Pass

Once you've a worked the foundation row, continue to alternate working forward and return passes.

Note: *Each vertical bar corresponds to one Tunisian simple stitch.*

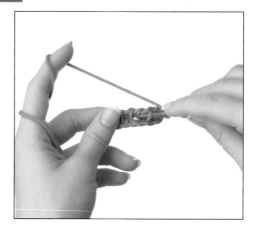

1. Skip the first vertical bar from the previous row. Insert your hook behind the next vertical bar. YO and draw up a loop.

2. Insert the hook behind the next vertical bar (see photo). YO and draw up a loop.

3. Repeat Step 2 until one stitch remains.

4. For the last stitch in the forward pass, insert the hook into both vertical bars at the end of the row. YO and draw up a loop.

   You now have as many loops on your hook as there are stitches in the previous row.

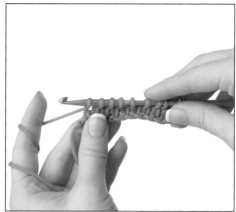

TIP

You can also try combining this technique with other crochet stitches. Try working the Foundation Forward Pass into a row of single crochet, just as you would work into the chain.

TSS Return Pass

Note: *You work the Tunisian simple stitch return pass with the right side of the work facing you. Do not turn the work.*

1. YO and draw the yarn through one loop on the hook.

2. YO and draw the yarn through two loops on the hook.

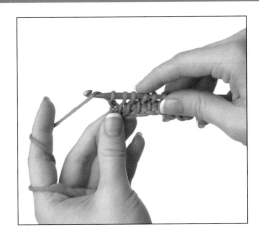

3. Repeat Step 2 until you reach the end of the return pass.

   At the end of this row, one loop remains on the hook.

CONTINUED ON NEXT PAGE

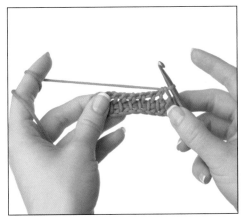

TIP

Different Tunisian crochet stitches can be created by varying where you insert your hook. For example, you can insert your hook under the horizontal bar to create a different texture.

TUNISIAN KNIT STITCH

The Tunisian knit stitch creates a fabric that looks much like the right side of knitted stockinette stitch. Its pattern abbreviation is Tks.

Forward Pass

1. Work a foundation pass as you would for Tunisian simple stitch. (See the preceding section, "Foundation Forward Pass.")

2. Skip the first stitch from the previous row. Working between 2 vertical bars, insert your hook from front to back under both horizontal strands (a).

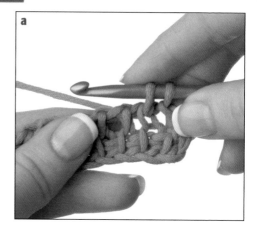

3. YO and draw the yarn through.

   There are now 2 loops on the hook.

4. Insert the hook from front to back under the next pair of horizontal strands (b). YO and draw the yarn through.

5. Repeat Step 3 until you have completed the forward row.

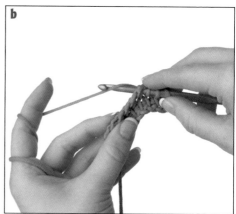

Return Pass

Note: *You work the Tunisian knit stitch return row with the right side of the work facing you. Do not turn the work.*

1 YO and draw the yarn through 1 loop on the hook (see photo).

2 YO and draw the yarn through 2 loops on the hook.

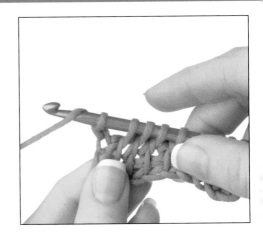

3 Repeat Step 2 until you reach the end of the return row.

There is now 1 loop on the hook.

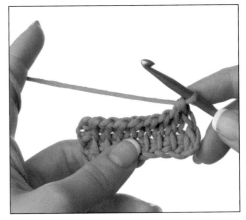

CONTINUED ON NEXT PAGE

TUNISIAN PURL STITCH

The Tunisian purl stitch creates a fabric that looks much like the wrong side of knitted stockinette stitch. Its pattern abbreviation is Tps.

Foundation Forward Pass

1. Make a chain equal to the number of stitches you require.

2. Holding the yarn in front of your work, insert the hook into the second chain (a).

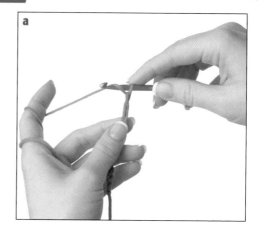

3. YO and draw the yarn through (b). There are now 2 loops on the hook.

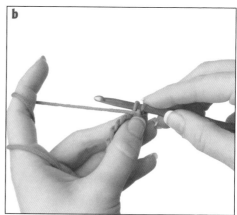

④ Holding the yarn in front of your work, insert the hook into the next chain and draw the yarn through.

There are now 3 loops on the hook (a).

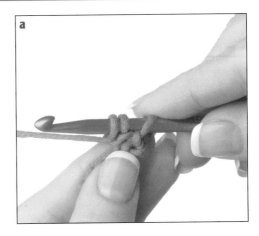

⑤ Repeat step 3 until you reach the end of the row. Do not turn your work.

You now have 1 loop on your hook for each chain (b).

Note: *There is a little purl bump for each loop.*

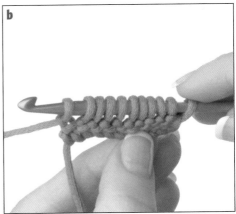

CONTINUED ON NEXT PAGE

Foundation Return Pass

Work the foundation return pass as you would for Tunisian simple stitch. (See the earlier section "Tunisian Simple Stitch.")

Forward Pass

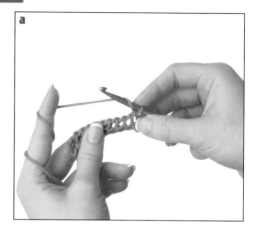

1. Skip the first stitch from the previous row. Hold your hook with the yarn in front of the work (a) and insert it behind the next vertical bar, as you would if you were working Tunisian simple stitch.

2. YO and draw the yarn through. There are now 2 loops on the hook.

3. Insert the hook behind the next vertical bar. YO and draw the yarn through. Repeat until 1 stitch remains.

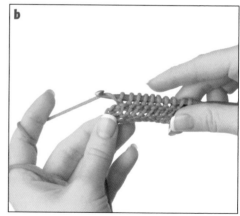

4. For the last stitch in the forward row, insert the hook into both vertical bars at the end of the row (b).

5. YO and draw the yarn through.

Return Pass

Work the return row as you would for Tunisian simple stitch.

BIND OFF IN TUNISIAN CROCHET

The final row of Tunisian crochet is worked differently from the rest of the piece. You work only a forward row, and you bind off stitches as you go, resulting in a neat, finished edge.

Bind Off

1. At the beginning of a forward row, insert your hook behind the second vertical bar. Yarn over and draw the yarn through.

   You now have 2 loops on your hook (a).

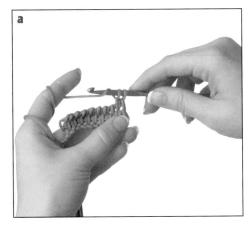

2. Yarn over and draw the yarn through both loops on the hook.

   You now have 1 loop on your hook. You have bound off 1 stitch.

3. *Insert your hook behind the next vertical bar. Yarn over and draw the yarn through. Yarn over and draw the yarn through both loops on the hook (b). Repeat from the * until the end of the row.

   You have 1 loop remaining on your hook.

4. Cut the yarn, leaving a 6-inch tail. Draw the yarn through the loop to fasten off.

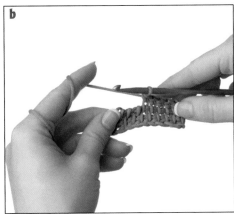

CONTINUED ON NEXT PAGE

COMPARING TUNISIAN SWATCHES

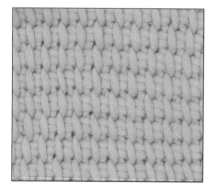

Tunisian Simple Stitch

Tunisian Knit Stitch

Tunisian Purl Stitch

Work with Color: Stranding

When the spaces between color changes are small, you can work one color and carry the other loosely across the wrong side of the fabric. This kind of color work creates a *right side* (a) and a *wrong side*—the side where the strands are hidden (b). The stranded yarn is always carried on the wrong side. Be careful of this as you turn your work with each row.

Secure stranded yarn every few stitches by working a stitch over the strand as you work.

If you catch the yarn securely enough, you can snip the strands and weave them in later to allow for better drape in your fabric.

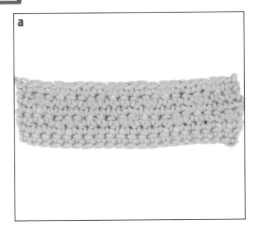

a

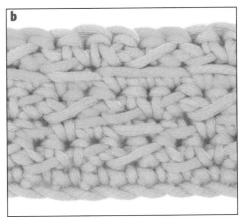

b

There is little difference between the front and back sides when a color pattern is worked in intarsia. Instead of stranding the unused yarn across the work, you can simply drop it and let it hang until you need it again.

This works well when the spaces between color changes are too large for stranding to be practical, when more than two yarns are in use, or if the nature of the stitch pattern won't accommodate stranding.

Each section of color in the design is worked from its own separate length of yarn. Many patterns list the precise amount of each color required; this is so you can make conveniently-sized small balls or bobbins of each color.

Work with Color: Tapestry Crochet

Tapestry crochet is used to create pieces with intricate color-work designs and motifs. This method is worked at a tight gauge and creates stiff fabric, perfect for baskets and bags.

Tapestry crochet designs and motifs are depicted in charts like this one, which depicts a seven-stitch pattern that can be repeated many times to create a motif like the example in the photo.

Tapestry crochet is often worked in rounds without turning. This means that the texture of the front and back sides of the rows don't alternate. This keeps the stitches slanting in the same direction and helps create a clear motif on the side facing you as you work—the "right side." The charted design is made with this in mind. To read the chart, read each row from right to left instead of alternating with each row.

Note: If you wish to work a motif in flat rows that was designed for a project in the round, you may need to make adjustments to the motif to account for the alternating slant of the stitches created by turning each row.

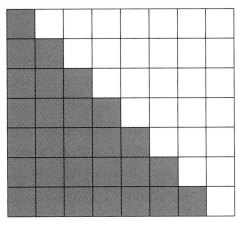

CONTINUED ON NEXT PAGE

The method for switching colors used in tapestry crochet is slightly different from the one described in Chapter 3. When you reach the last stitch of a section of color in the pattern, work the last stitch to the final step. Pick up the next color in the pattern, and yarn over with only this yarn to complete the stitch (see the photo). This completed stitch will look a bit funny, with the top of the stitch in the new color and the bottom half in the previous color.

Though traditionally made with cotton thread and a steel crochet hook, modern interpretations of the technique have been worked in thicker yarns with larger hooks.

Filet crochet designs are created in positive and negative space, and are depicted in charts in which each filet block represents one square of the grid. Open and filled blocks are used to create patterns of shapes. See Chapter 5 for more on how to follow a chart.

To follow a chart, read the chart beginning from the bottom right. Odd-numbered rows are read from right to left; even-numbered rows are read from left to right.

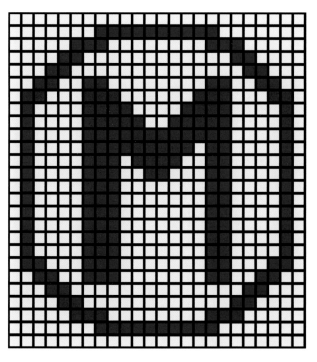

CONTINUED ON NEXT PAGE

Filet Crochet
(continued)

WORK AN OPEN BLOCK

An open block consists of [CH 2, 1 DC] over three stitches (or the foundation chain) from the previous row.

① Where you want the block to begin, CH 2, skip 2 stitches, work one dc into the next dc.

② Repeat Step 1 until the chart calls for a filled block.

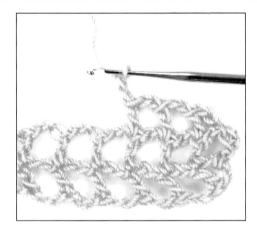

WORK A FILLED BLOCK

A filled block consists of three DC over three stitches (or the foundation chain) from the previous row.

If you're working into an open block from the previous row:

> Work two DC into the next CH-2 space, work one DC into the next DC.

If you're working into a filled block from the previous row:

> Work one DC into each of the next three DC.

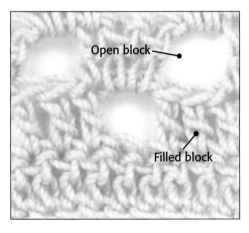

Open block

Filled block

Crochet with Beads

THREAD BEADS ON YARN

Patterns calling for bead crochet will specify the quantity and size of beads required. Thread all the beads you need onto the yarn before you begin to crochet.

1 Fold a piece of thread over the yarn tail.

   This folded piece of thread works as a flexible needle. Think of the ends of the thread as the point of a needle.

2 Slide beads onto the thread "needle" and then onto the yarn.

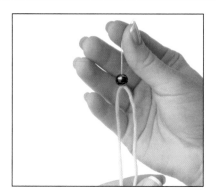

WORK A BEAD INTO A STITCH

Beads can be worked into any crochet stitch; this example uses single crochet.

1 Before completing the final step of any stitch, slide a bead close to your hook.

2 Yarn over and pull through to complete the stitch. This step secures a bead in the stitch.

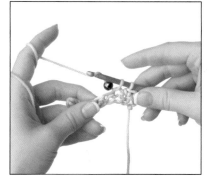

The bead sits on the side of the fabric facing away from you as you work the row.

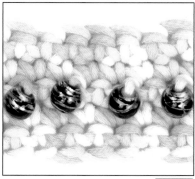

Broomstick Loops

You can work these loops into any stitch. Start with a chain or row of any length. An actual broomstick is not necessary; a large knitting needle works well for this stitch. The larger the "broomstick," the larger the loops.

Right-handed: Work from left to right, with the hook in the right hand and the broomstick in your left hand.

Left-handed: Work from right to left, with the hook in the left hand and the broomstick in your right hand.

1 Without turning your work, insert the hook into the next stitch from the previous row, yarn over, and draw up a loop, lengthening the loop so that it can be placed on the broomstick.

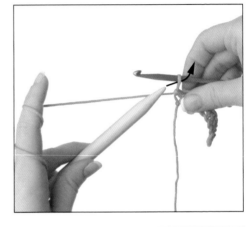

Leave the loop on the broomstick. Repeat across the row.

Note: *At the end of a row of broomstick loops, the loops are still on the broomstick. The next row locks these loops in place so they don't unravel.*

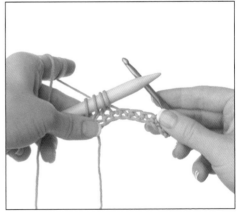

2 Slip one loop off the broomstick and onto the hook.

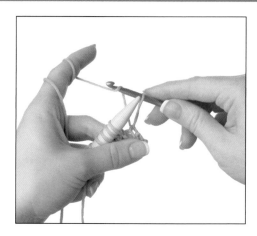

3 YO and draw the yarn through both loops on the hook. CH 1.

4 Repeat Steps 2 and 3, working into every loop across the row.

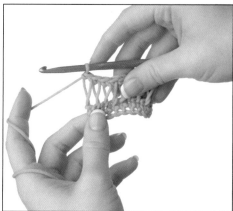

Hairpin lace uses single crochet stitches to secure loops of yarn around a loom consisting of two wooden or metal prongs attached at the top and bottom. It's a technique all on its own, but is often considered a subset of crochet. You make strips of hairpin lace, then attach the strips into unique looking garments or other items.

The loops on a basic strip can be twisted and worked up in all sorts of ways to create unique lace textures. Here we only focus on the basic strip, any pattern you work with will instruct you on how to combine the strips. If you're just trying out the technique, the basic strip worked with the right yarn or combination of yarns makes a cool scarf.

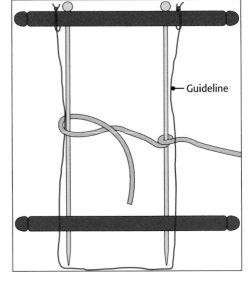

Guideline

SET UP THE LOOM AND GET STARTED

Set the prongs of the loom to the desired width. Before placing the bottom on the loom, use a loose slip knot to attach the yarn to one of the prongs. Leaving the loop loose, center the knot on the prong.

You'll use one hand to hold the hook and one to control the yarn. Use the yarn hand to hold the loom too. You may wish to work with the loom on your lap. Start with the slip knot on the prong on the yarn hand side of the loom. The examples in this section feature the left hand as the yarn hand and the right hand as the hook hand.

To manage the strip as it goes, tie on a guideline. With a piece of yarn twice the length you plan the strip to be, tie the yarn at the top of the loom, run alongside the prong, through the slip knot loop, across the bottom of the loom and back up the other prong and tie the end to the top of the loom (see illustration for guideline). If you're planning to make a long strip, the guideline will hang past the loom; wrap the excess guideline on itself until needed (see final photo).

WORK THE FIRST STITCH

1 Wrap the yarn across the front of the loom (over, not behind, the opposite prong) and to the back. The yarn will be hanging in the back middle. Insert your hook up through the slip knot loop, grab the yarn with the hook and draw a loop through the slip knot loop; CH 1. To keep track of the start, mark this stitch.

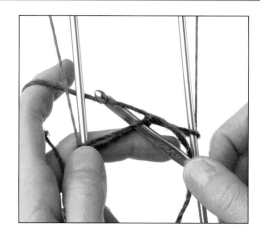

2 Do not remove the hook from the loop. Rotate the hook, parallel with the prongs, with the hook pointing down and the handle pointing up. Tilt the handle through the loom and grab the hook from the back of loom.

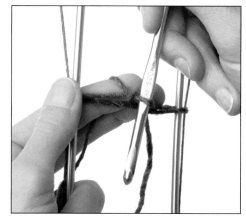

CONTINUED ON NEXT PAGE

❸ Flip the loom toward your yarn hand, allowing the yarn to wrap around. The marked prong is now on the opposite side, your hook is in position, and the yarn is in your yarn hand at back of loom.

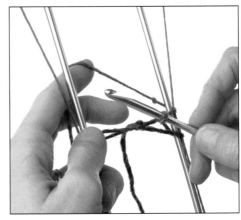

SINGLE CROCHET

❹ Insert the hook into the loop space closest to the top of the loom. YO and draw a loop through the loop space, YO, and pull yarn through two loops to make 1 sc.

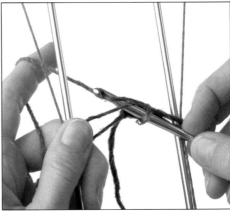

TIP

There are many different ways to join strips of hairpin lace; if you're working with a pattern, it should provide those instructions. Here is a simple way similar to working a crochet seam (see Chapter 6): Align two strips of hairpin lace with the beginning of each strip to the left side. Lay one strip on top of the other with loops from each strip lined up with each other. Work a single crochet two loops together by inserting the hook through the first loop of each strip. Continue to work single crochet through the loops across the two strips.

5 Continue to work, repeating the steps to flip the loom and work a sc.

Note: Keep work pushed down on the loom to allow room to maneuver the hook. When the loom is too full for comfort, remove the bottom of the loom and slide all but the newest loops off the loom. Replace the bottom and roll up the loose hairpin lace. You can use a rubber band or stitch holders to secure the rolled lace.

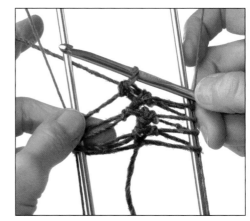

6 To fasten off, leave a tail. Cut the yarn and draw through the last loop.

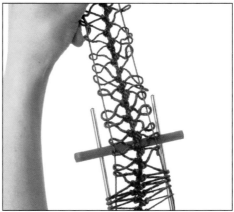

Easy to make, this simple daisy makes a sweet addition to any project. Use it as an appliqué, make it into a pin, or even use it to patch up a pair of old jeans. The example was made with DK weight yarn and a 4.5 mm hook. You can use any yarn to make your own simple daisies; choose a hook size appropriate for the yarn you've chosen.

STITCHES USED

CH	Chain stitch
Sl st	Slip stitch
SC	Single crochet
DC	Double crochet

Note: See Chapter 2 for more on how to make these stitches.

FOUNDATION ROUND

① CH 2. Work 5 SC into the second CH from the hook. Join with a sl st. Gently pull on the tail to tighten the ring.

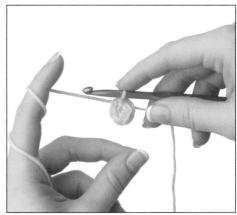

PETAL ROUND

Each petal is made by using a combination of stitches worked into 1 SC.

1 Starting in the first SC from the previous round, [CH 2, 3 DC, CH 2, sl st]. You have made one petal.

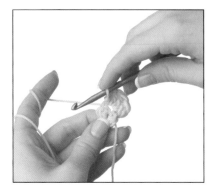

2 *Sl st into the next SC Work 1 petal [CH 2, 3 DC, CH 2, sl st] into this SC.

3 Repeat from * to create a total of 5 petals. Sl st to join at the base of the first petal.

4 Tie off and weave in the ends.

Note: Instead of weaving in the yarn tails, you can use them to sew the daisy onto a crocheted project or tie it onto a pin.

Increasing by too many stitches in each row creates a ruffle in a row. Increasing by *far* too many stitches causes the work to turn in on itself, resulting in a playful corkscrew that makes a playful fringe or ornament. The example was made with DK weight yarn and a 4.5 mm hook. You can use any yarn to make your own corkscrews; choose a hook size appropriate for the yarn you've chosen.

STITCHES USED

CH   Chain stitch

Sl st   Slip stitch

SC   Single crochet

See Chapter 2 for more on how to make these stitches.

CORKSCREW PATTERN

1. CH any number—the longer the chain, the longer the corkscrew.

2. Sl st into the second CH from the hook. *Work 4 SC into the next CH (see photo).

3. Repeat from *, working into each CH across.

Teardrop

This simple motif works up quickly. The unusual shape adds interest to any project as an appliqué or as motifs that are joined. The example was made with DK weight yarn and a 4.5 mm hook. Any yarn can be used; choose a hook size appropriate for the yarn you've chosen.

STITCHES USED

CH	Chain stitch
Sl st	Slip stitch
SC	Single crochet
DC	Double crochet
TR	Treble crochet
DTR	Double treble

See Chapters 2 and 4 for more on how to make these stitches.

TEARDROP PATTERN

1. CH 6. Sl st to join the first chain to the last for working in the round. CH 1.

2. Working into the center of the ring, make 3 SC, 1 DC, 3 TR, CH 1, 1 DTR, CH 1, 3 TR, 1 DC, 3 SC (see photo).

3. Sl st into the first SC at the beginning of the round to join. Tie off.

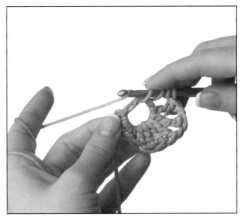

Triangles Using Increases or Decreases

Use simple shaping techniques to create a triangle shape. Start with a point and increase as you go, or start with a long row and decrease to a point. The example was made with DK weight yarn and a 4.5 mm hook. Any yarn can be used; choose a hook size appropriate for the yarn you've chosen.

STITCHES USED

CH	Chain stitch
Sl st	Slip stitch
SC	Single crochet
SC2TOG	Single crochet together

Note: *See Chapter 2 for more on how to make these stitches. Also, see Chapter 3 for more on increasing and decreasing.*

DECREASE TRIANGLE

1. CH any number plus 1 for the turning CH.

2. Row 1: Work 1 SC into the second loop from the hook. Work 1 SC into each CH across. CH 1 and turn.

3. Row 2: Work SC2TOG over the next 2 sts from the previous row. Work 1 SC into each st across to finish the row. CH 1 and turn.

4. Repeat Row 2 to decrease 1 st per row until only 3 sts are left.

5. Final row: SC3TOG to complete the triangle. Tie off.

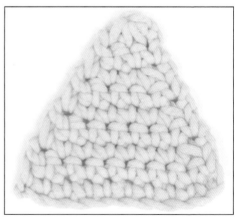

INCREASE TRIANGLE

1. CH 2.

2. Row 1: Work 3 SC into the second CH from the hook. CH 1 and turn.

3. Row 2: Work 2 SC into the first st of the previous row. Work 1 SC in each st across to finish the row. CH 1 and turn.

4. Repeat Row 2 until the triangle is the desired size.

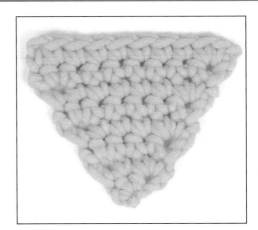

TIP

Appliqué triangles to completed projects for a playful look, especially for children's items. Consider making a large triangle to use as a head scarf, dish rag, or face cloth.

Triangle in the Round

Instead of making a triangle by increasing from a point or decreasing to a point (see previous section), you can easily work one up by crocheting in the round. The example was made with DK weight yarn and a 4.5 mm hook. Any yarn can be used; choose a hook size appropriate for the yarn you've chosen.

STITCHES USED

CH   Chain stitch

Sl st   Slip stitch

DC   Double crochet

See Chapter 2 for more on how to make these stitches. Also, see the section "Create a Ring Using a Loop" in Chapter 3.

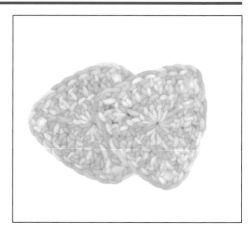

TRIANGLE PATTERN

1 Round 1: Using a loop to form a ring, CH 3 and work 4 DC into the ring. *CH 2, work 5 DC. Repeat from * once to complete the round. CH 2, sl st in the third CH of the CH 3 at the beginning of the round to join. Pull on the tail of the loop to tighten the center.

2 Round 2: CH 3; this chain counts as 1 DC. Skip the first DC from the previous round. *Work 1 DC into each DC from the previous round until you reach the first CH space. Work [1 DC, CH 2, 1 DC] into the CH space. Repeat from * twice to complete the round. Sl st in the third CH of the CH 3 at the beginning of the round.

3 Repeat Round 2 until the triangle is the desired size.

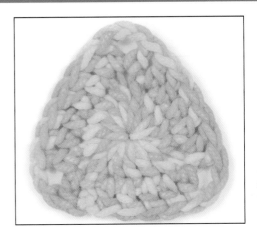

TIP

To turn the triangle motif into a triangle box, follow the motif pattern to create the base of the box. To shape the sides of the box, work 1 SC in front loop only of each DC of the previous round and [1 SC, Ch 2, 1 SC] into the CH 2 space of the previous round; join the round with a slip stitch. For each round after that, work 1 SC in each stitch from the previous round, joining the rounds with a slip stitch.

Rectangle in the Round

This motif is worked in the round instead of in rows to create an interesting fabric of concentric rectangles. The example in this tutorial was made with DK weight yarn and a 4.5 mm hook. Any yarn can be used; choose a hook size appropriate for the yarn you've chosen.

STITCHES USED

CH   Chain stitch

Sl st   Slip stitch

DC   Double crochet

See Chapter 2 for more on how to make these stitches.

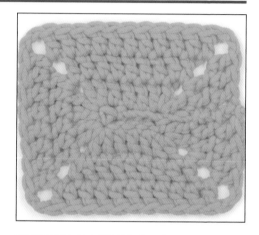

RECTANGLE PATTERN

① CH 6.

② Round 1: Working into the top loop of the CH braid, work a sl st into the second CH from the hook and into every CH until the last CH. Work 2 sl st in the last CH to turn the corner. Continue to work into the back side of the CH, working 1 sl st into both remaining loops of each CH across the backside.

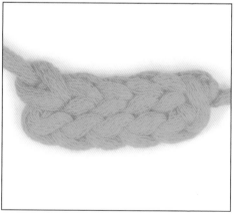

3 Round 2: CH 3; this chain counts as a DC. Work 1 DC into the first st of the round, CH 1, 2 DC into the next st. Work 1 DC into each of the next 3 sts. Work [2 DC in the next st, CH 1, 2 DC in the next] to create a corner.

4 Work [2 DC in the next st, CH 1, 2 DC in the next st] to create another corner. Work 1 DC into each of the next 3 sts. Work [2 DC in the next st, CH 1, 2 DC in the next st] to create another corner. Sl st to the third CH of the CH 3 from the beginning of the round.

5 Round 3: CH 3; this chain counts as 1 DC. Skip the first DC from the previous round. *Work 1 DC into each DC from the previous round until the CH space; work [1 DC, CH 2, 1 DC] into the CH space.

6 Repeat from * 3 times. Work 1 DC into each DC from the previous round. Sl st in the third CH of the CH 3 at the beginning of the round.

7 Repeat Round 3 until the rectangle is the desired size.

TIP

It's simple to make changes to this rectangle. Try starting with a longer chain for a longer center. You could also try starting with a row of foundation single crochet. Simply work Round 2 into both sides of the foundation single crochet.

Mitered Square

A mitered square starts with a straight row that bends 90 degrees as you decrease in the center of each row. This is a fun way to make a square with an interesting look. The example was made with DK weight yarn and a 4.5 mm hook. You can use any yarn to make your own mitered squares; choose a hook size appropriate for the yarn you've chosen.

STITCHES USED

CH   Chain stitch

Sl st   Slip stitch

SC   Single crochet

See Chapter 2 for more on how to make these stitches.

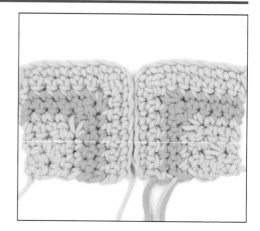

MITERED SQUARE PATTERN

1. Create a foundation chain that is an odd number, plus 1 for the turning chain.

2. Row 1: Work 1 SC in the second CH and each CH across. CH 1 and turn. Place a stitch marker in the st at the center of the row.

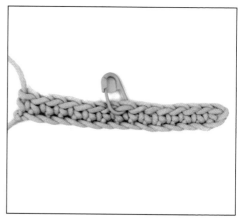

3 Row 2: Work 1 SC in each st across to the st before the marker. Remove the marker. Work 3 SC TOG over the center 3 sts. Work 1 SC into each st across to the end of the row, CH 1, and turn. Move the marker to the st at the center of the row.

4 Repeat Row 2 until 3 sts are left in the row.

5 Final row: Work 3 SC TOG. Tie off and weave in ends.

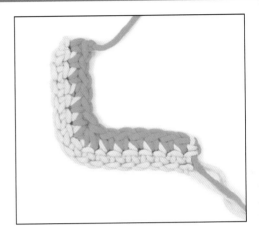

TIP

Mitered squares may be combined to create intricate patterns. Use the squares as building blocks to create larger designs. Changing colors and using stripes are key in making these kinds of combinations. For a simple, but different approach to making a blanket, consider working one blanket-sized mitered square.

Pentagon

Pentagons are perfect for piecing together into scarves or afghans. They're just as simple to crochet as circles but add a bit of variety. The example in this tutorial was made with DK weight yarn and a 4.5 mm hook. Any yarn can be used; choose a hook size appropriate for the yarn you've chosen.

STITCHES USED

CH   Chain stitch

Sl st   Slip stitch

DC   Double crochet

Note: *See Chapter 2 for more on how to make these stitches. Also, see the section "Create a Ring Using a Loop" in Chapter 3.*

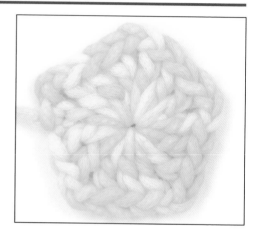

PENTAGON PATTERN

① Round 1: Using a loop for a ring, CH 3 and work 2 DC into the ring. *CH 2, work 3 DC. Repeat from * 4 times. CH 2, Sl st in the third CH of the CH 3 at the beginning of the round to join. Pull on the tail of the loop to tighten the center.

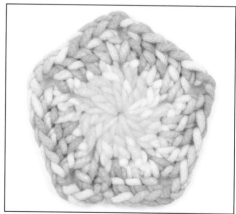

2 Round 2: CH 3; this chain counts as 1 DC. Skip the first DC from the previous round. Work 1 DC into each DC from the previous round until you reach the first CH space. Work [1 DC, CH 2, 1 DC] into the CH space. *Work 1 DC into each DC; work [1 DC, CH 2, 1 DC] into the CH space. Repeat from * 5 times to complete the round. Sl st in the third CH of the CH 3 at the beginning of the round.

3 Repeat Round 2 until the pentagon is the desired size.

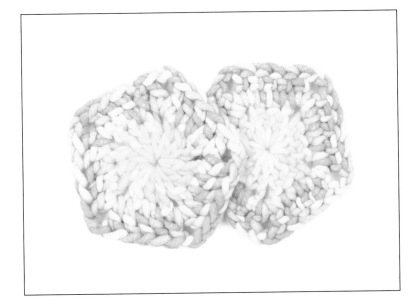

TIP

It's easy to make a hexagon or octagon following the same idea. Simply add more sides to your motif by adding another CH 2, 3 DC repeat for each side you wish to add. For example: To get an octagon started, work the CH 2, 3 DC repeat in Round 1 seven times.

The traditional granny square has survived the decades because it's fun to make and easy to modify to suit your preferences.

SPECIAL STITCH COMBINATIONS

Granny cluster: 3 DC in CH-1 space

Corner set: [3 DC, CH 2, 3 DC] in CH-2 space

Note: *See Chapter 2 for more on how to make these stitches. Also, see Chapter 3.*

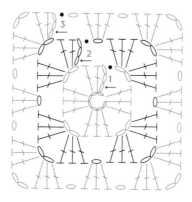

Use the chart along with the pattern text to get a better understanding of what the pattern wants you to do. Once you have the hang of it, the chart is a handy visual aid—easy to glance at as you crochet. To follow the chart, start at the center and follow the arrows to work your way around.

MAKE A GRANNY SQUARE

1. **Round 1:** Using a loop for a ring, CH 3 and work 2 DC into the ring. *CH 2, 3 DC into the ring. Repeat from * twice to create two more granny clusters. CH 2, sl st in the third CH of the CH-3 at the beginning of the round. Fasten off. Tighten the ring.

2. **Round 2:** Join the yarn (see Chapter 3) in the next CH-2 space. Work [CH 3, 2 DC, CH 2, 3 DC] into the CH space (see photo). *CH 1. In the next CH space, work a corner set [3 DC, CH 2, 3 DC]. Repeat from * to work a corner set into each CH-2 space. CH 1, sl st in the third CH of the CH-3 at the beginning of the round. Fasten off.

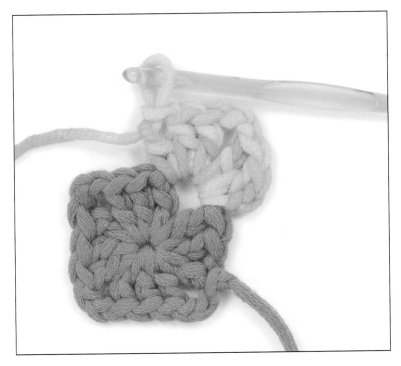

CONTINUED ON NEXT PAGE

3 Round 3: Join the yarn in the next corner CH space. Work [CH 3, 2 DC, CH 2, 3 DC] into the CH space. *CH 1. Work one granny cluster in each CH-1 space; CH 1. In the next CH-2 space, work a corner set [3 DC, CH 2, 3 DC].

4 Repeat from * to work into each CH space, ending with CH 1, granny cluster in the last CH-1 space. CH 1, sl st in the third CH of the CH-3 at the beginning of the round. Fasten off.

Note: *From here, the number of granny clusters worked into CH spaces between corner sets increases with each round. Also, to join new colors, first attach the new yarn to your hook using a slip knot. Join the yarn to a corner CH space with a slip stitch, and continue with the pattern.*

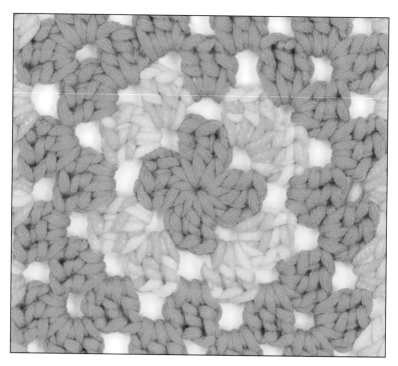

WHAT YOU CAN DO WITH GRANNY SQUARES

Granny squares are easy, cheery, and quick to stitch. Combine a rich yarn with sweet colors and you can create all sorts of items, from afghans, ponchos, and scarves, to bags that are both old-fashioned and irresistibly chic—such as the one shown here.

chapter 6

Finishing

When the crocheting is done, several steps remain before a project is complete. This chapter covers the final steps of finishing, blocking, and embellishing.

Buttonholes

Here are two basic methods for making a buttonhole to fit any button. Use the first technique to make a horizontal buttonhole within a row of crochet. Use the second technique to make a vertical buttonhole over two or more rows of crochet.

MAKE A BUTTONHOLE WITHIN A ROW

① Work up to the point where you will insert a buttonhole. CH 3, skip 3 stitches, and continue in pattern to the end of the row. Make a turning chain and turn.

Note: We used a three-stitch buttonhole for this example. Depending on the size of your button, you may need to make your buttonhole larger or smaller. Simply compare the button to the buttonhole to make sure that it's a good fit. Adjust the number of skipped stitches and chains as needed so that the buttonhole is slightly smaller than the button.

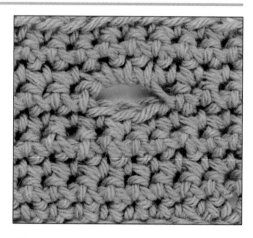

② Work the next row according to the pattern, working 3 stitches as called for into the CH-3 space.

MAKE A BUTTONHOLE ACROSS ROWS

1. Work to the point where you will insert a buttonhole. Make a turning chain and turn.

2. Work back to the beginning of your work. Make a turning chain and turn.

3. Work to the end of the short row and fasten off.

4. Join the yarn one stitch from the end of the first short row (see photo). * Work in pattern to the end of the short row. Make a turning chain and turn.

5. Repeat from * twice.

6. Work in pattern to the end of the short row. CH 1. Work the next stitch into the last stitch from Step 3. Continue to the end of the row, work a turning chain, and turn. You've made a vertical buttonhole (see photo).

TIP

To sew a button onto crochet fabric, use a needle and thread just as you would on other fabric, but work the needle through one or more loops of the crochet fabric.

Sewing in a zipper, by hand or by machine, is an excellent skill to have. Use a zipper appropriate for the size of the opening in your project. If your piece features open lace, work rows of solid crochet where the zipper will be attached. If you're sewing a zipper into a bag or other item that will be seamed closed on three sides, attach the zipper before seaming.

① With wrong sides facing and using contrasting yarn, baste the crocheted edges closed using a whipstitch so that they lay flat and do not overlap.

② Lay the right side of the zipper face-down on top of the wrong side of the basted opening, aligning the center of the zipper with the opening. Pin the zipper in place using straight pins or baste it in place using sewing thread in a contrasting color.

3 If you're using a sewing machine (do so only if the project can lay flat), sew the zipper to the garment. If you're sewing by hand (required for projects that are already closed on two or more sides), use a running stitch or backstitch to sew the zipper to the garment.

4 Remove the pins or basting. On the wrong side, whipstitch the flat sides of the zipper to the crocheted fabric so they lay flat. Turn out the project so the right side is facing.

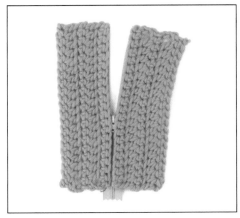

TIP

Be careful if you choose to use a sewing machine to sew your zipper. Bulky fabric can cause trouble for a machine, and a sewing machine may damage your crocheted fabric. Sewing a zipper by hand doesn't take too long!

Patch Pockets

Patch pockets are simple to crochet and simple to add to any project. They're functional and decorative.

1. Crochet a square, semicircle, or rectangle to serve as the pocket.

2. On the garment or accessory, use a pin or stitch marker to mark the placement of the pocket. If you're working on a garment, you might want to try it on to ensure proper placement

3. Sew the left, right, and bottom sides of the pocket to the right side of the project with a whipstitch, being sure to secure the top corners to prevent separation during wear and use.

There are many ways to join motifs such as granny squares or flowers together into a whole. Squares can be joined with any seam; chains can be used to create a very decorative join.

JOIN MOTIFS SOLIDLY

Whipstitch or a woven seam are often used to join motifs. See the "Seaming" section for more information.

To create a less bulky whipstitch seam, insert the yarn needle through only the "inside" loops of the edge stitches only.

Single crochet and slip stitch can be used to create a decorative seam appropriate for some afghans or other home décor projects involving motifs.

CONTINUED ON NEXT PAGE

JOIN MOTIFS USING CHAINS

Use chains to create an open-work, decorative join.

① Lay two motifs side by side on a flat surface with right sides facing.

② Join matching yarn with sl st to lower corner stitch of one piece. CH 3.

③ Skip 3 edge stitches of other piece, sl st in next edge stitch. CH 3.

④ Repeat Step 3.

> **Note:** *We used 3 chains in our example. You can use any number of chains, and skip a number of stitches appropriate for the pattern of your motif.*

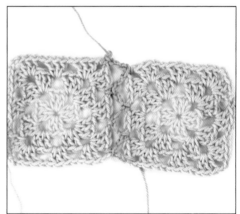

Pompoms are a playful addition to crocheted items, especially for kids. Place them on top of hats, at the ends of cords, or anywhere else that could use a little pizzazz.

1 Cut two pieces of cardboard into circles the same size you want your pompom to be. Cut a pie-shaped wedge out of each piece; then cut a circle out of the center of each of the pieces. The two pieces should be identical.

2 Lay a strand of yarn in a full circle over one of the cardboard pieces. Lay the second piece of cardboard over this yarn, sandwiching the yarn between the two pieces of cardboard.

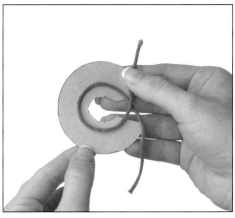

CONTINUED ON NEXT PAGE

③ Holding the two pieces of cardboard together, wrap yarn around the cardboard until it's too densely wrapped to take any more yarn.

④ Cut the yarn leaving a short tail. Using sharp scissors, cut the yarn between the two circles by inserting the scissors under the yarn and between the two cardboard pieces.

Tie the yarn sandwiched between the two cardboard circles into a very tight knot to secure the pompom. Remove the cardboard.

⑤ Trim the ends of the pompoms so they are uniform and neat.

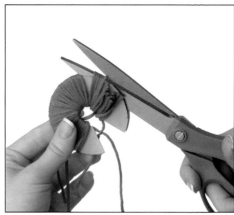

TIP

Make a multicolored pompom! Simply drop one color and start wrapping with another.

For yarn scraps shorter than a few feet, tie the scraps together to make one length of funky mismatched yarn. Use this scrap yarn to make unique pompoms and fringe.

Fringe is most often used to adorn afghans and scarves, but you can use fringe creatively to add a playful or elegant detail to hats, shawls, belts, and more.

CUT FRINGE

1. Cut a piece of cardboard that is slightly longer than the fringe you want to make. The piece of cardboard should be at least 3 to 4 inches wide.

   Note: A CD jewel case works well, too, as pictured in the photo below.

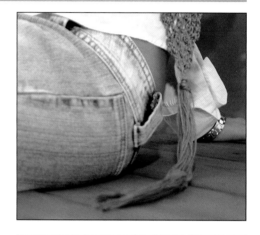

2. Wrap the yarn around the cardboard or jewel case. This ensures that all pieces of the fringe are the same length without you having to measure each strand.

3. Secure a rubber band around the yarn to keep the pieces in place. Cut the yarn along the bottom of the cardboard or jewel case. Keep the yarn folded in half.

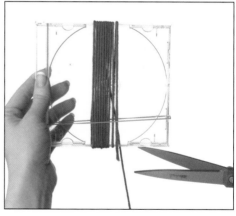

CONTINUED ON NEXT PAGE

ATTACH FRINGE

4 Insert a large crochet hook from back to front through the stitch to which you want to add fringe. Grab the middle of the folded fringe yarn with the hook and bring it through the stitch about 1 inch.

5 Keeping the hook inserted through the center of the fringe, use it to grab the entire bunch of fringe.

6 Draw the fringe through the loop and tighten.

7 Trim the ends of the fringe so that they're even.

TIP

There are limitless ways to add flair with your fringe. For full, thick fringe, attach several strands of fringe to the fabric in groups instead of individual strands. Consider combining colors and different textures for a lush fringe.

SINGLE-CROCHET EDGING

Working a row of single crochet stitches around a finished piece creates a neat, flat border.

1. Attach the yarn to the hook with a slip knot and join to any stitch of the piece using slip stitch.

2. Work a single crochet stitch into each stitch or row across. Work two to three single crochets into the corner stitch; adjust as needed to make sure the corner doesn't curl.

3. Repeat Step 2 until you've completed your border. Slip stitch in the first stitch of the edging. Fasten off and weave in the ends.

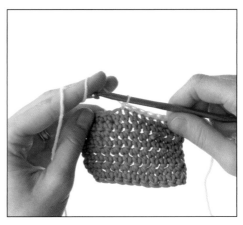

CONTINUED ON NEXT PAGE

TIP

Work a single crochet edging in a new color to add a subtle or vibrant design element to your work. You can also use slip stitch to make an even subtler, tighter edging.

PICOT EDGING

1. Attach the yarn to the hook with a slip knot and join to any corner of the piece using sl st.

2. Work 1 SC into the next stitch.

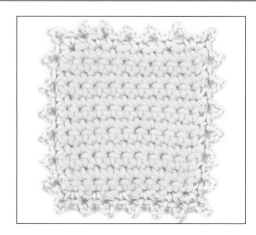

3. CH 3, sl st into the first CH (1 picot made).

4. Skip 1 stitch, SC into the next stitch.

5. Repeat Steps 3 and 4 to create a picot edging.

TIP

Work five chains to create a larger picot. You may need to skip two stitches before working the next single crochet to make the edging lie flat. Experiment!

CRAB STITCH EDGING

Crab stitch, also called *reverse single crochet* (rsc), is often used to create a simple, decorative border around a crocheted piece. Crab stitch is worked in the reverse direction from all other crochet stitches.

Note: *You can work the crab stitch onto fabric composed of any kind of stitch. Do not turn your work or make a turning chain.*

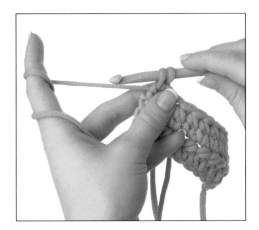

1 Insert your hook into the next stitch to the right (if you're left-handed, insert your hook into the next stitch to the left).

2 YO and draw up a loop. Two loops are now on the hook.

3 Draw the yarn through the 2 loops on your hook as you would if you were working a single crochet. You have made one crab stitch.

CONTINUED ON NEXT PAGE

TIP

Did you notice that the top of a crab stitch doesn't look like the top of other crochet stitches? This is why this stitch is only used as a border.

④ Continue to make crab stitches by inserting your hook into the next stitch in the opposite direction from normal. When you reach the end of the row, do not turn your work.

⑤ Work 2 crab stitches into the corner stitch to turn the corner (see photo).

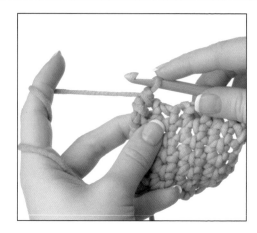

⑥ When you reach the first crab stitch of the edging, sl st into it to join the round. Fasten off and weave in the ends.

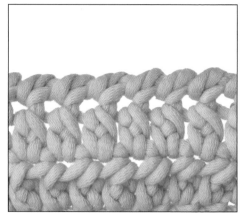

TIP

The crab stitch is a bit tighter than single crochet. Be careful to work the stitches at the right tension so as not to warp the fabric.

Blocking

Crocheted pieces made from natural fibers like cotton, wool, and silk look their best after they've been blocked to the proper shape and dimensions. Blocking also helps make stitches look uniform and even. You can block all the pieces of a project before you assemble them (this is often recommended), or you can assemble and then block.

SPRAY AND STEAM BLOCKING

You need a firm, flat surface to serve as a blocking board on which to pin your pieces. You can use a bed, lay several towels on a table or carpet, or use a large Styrofoam board.

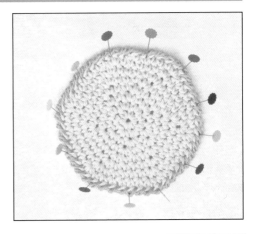

❶ Lay out your crocheted pieces on your blocking board (as shown in photo). Using your pattern as a guide, pin the pieces to the required shape and dimensions.

Be sure to use rustproof pins.

❷ **Spray blocking:** If spray blocking use a spray bottle to wet the pieces thoroughly with tepid water.

CONTINUED ON NEXT PAGE

Steam blocking: If steam blocking, use the steam from an iron or a steamer held several inches above the pieces.

Allow the pieces to dry, possibly overnight. Remove the pins.

Note: *Some synthetic yarns do not hold up well under high heat. Test a swatch before doing a full steam blocking.*

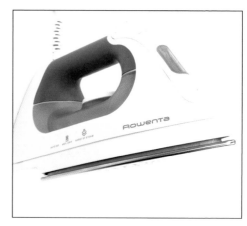

WET BLOCK

1. Gently submerge your crocheted piece(s) in cool water (add mild soap or wool wash to clean, if desired). Do not agitate. Allow the piece(s) to soak for 10 to 15 minutes. Drain the sink. Gently squeeze excess water from the piece(s). Use a towel to gently roll more water out of the piece(s), as shown in the photo.

2. Lay the pieces out on your blocking board as directed for steam and spray blocking. Allow to dry thoroughly.

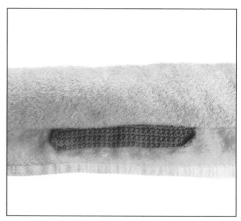

Unless your pattern specifically called for it, do not under any circumstances iron your crocheted pieces.

You can use one of several sewing techniques to attach crocheted pieces to each other.

WHIPSTITCH SEAM

1 Hold together the two pieces to be seamed, with their right sides together and with stitches or rows matched up (see photo).

Note: The right side is the side that shows when the garment is worn. The wrong side is the side that is hidden. When right sides are held facing each other for seaming, the piece will later be turned right side out, hiding the seam on the inside.

2 Using matching yarn or thread and a yarn needle, insert the needle from back to front through the first stitch or row of each piece, leaving a 6-inch tail.

3 Bringing the needle over the top of the work, insert it from back to front through the next pair of stitches (see photo).

Repeat Step 3 to the end of the seam. Fasten off and weave in the yarn tails.

CONTINUED ON NEXT PAGE

BACKSTITCH SEAM

Backstitch creates a sturdy seam and is suited for use on curved or angled edges.

1 Hold the two pieces to be seamed with their right sides together and with stitches or rows matched up. Using matching yarn or thread and a yarn needle, insert the needle from front to back through the first stitch or row of each piece.

2 Insert the needle from back to front through the next pair of stitches.

3 Insert the needle from front to back through the first pair of stitches again.

4 Skipping the next pair of stitches, insert the needle from back to front through the pair of stitches beyond.

5 Insert the needle from front to back into the preceding pair of stitches.

6 Skipping one pair of stitches, insert the needle from back to front into the next pair of stitches.

7 Repeat Steps 5 and 6 to the end of the seam. Fasten off and weave in the ends (see photo).

TIP

The tension of the seam will affect the look of the finished piece. You'll want your seam stitches to be snug, not too loose or too tight.

WOVEN SEAM

A woven seam (also referred to as *mattress stitch*) is suitable for use only when seaming stitches to stitches (not stitches to row ends or row ends to row ends). It is popular for joining motifs because it is an invisible seam.

1 Hold together the two pieces to be seamed with their right sides together and with stitches matched up. Using matching yarn or thread and a yarn needle, insert the needle into the center of the top of the first stitch or row of one piece and pull the yarn through.

2 Insert the needle into the center of the top of the first stitch on the other piece and pull the yarn through loosely.

3 Continue to alternate from one piece to the other, tightening the seam every few inches.

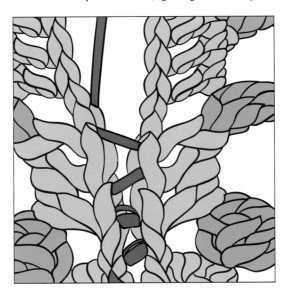

Use slip stitch or single crochet as an alternative to sewing. These techniques create sturdy and optionally decorative seams.

CREATE A SLIP STITCH SEAM

Slip stitch is suited for use on irregularly shaped edges. It creates a strong seam.

1. Hold the two pieces to be seamed with their right sides together and with stitches or rows matched up.

   Note: See Tip on page 157 for more on right and wrong sides.

2. Using matching yarn (we used a contrasting yarn here in the photo for clarity) and an appropriately sized crochet hook, insert the hook from front to back through both loops of each of the first pair of stitches, or through each of the first pair of rows.

3. YO and draw the yarn through and through the loop on the hook, creating 1 sl st.

   Repeat Steps 2 and 3 to the end of the seam, working into the next pair of stitches or rows. Fasten off and weave in the tails.

CREATE A SINGLE CROCHET SEAM

① Hold the two pieces to be seamed with their right sides together and with stitches or rows matched up.

Alternatively, you can work this seam with the wrong sides together, to have the seam show decoratively on the right side.

② Using matching yarn and an appropriately sized crochet hook, insert the hook from front to back through both loops of each of the first pair of stitches, or through each of the first pair of rows (see photo).

③ YO and draw the yarn through both stitches. YO again and draw the yarn through both loops on the hook, creating 1 SC.

④ Repeat Steps 2 and 3 to the end of the seam, working into the next pair of stitches or rows. Fasten off and weave in the tails.

TIP

A single crochet seam is bulky and not well suited to garments. It does make a great strong seam for bags. For a ridge similar to piping, use a slip stitch or single crochet seam worked with the wrong sides together so the seam will show on the right side.

Care for Crocheted Items

After all the time, energy, and love involved in making crocheted items, it's important to care for them properly so that they remain in excellent condition for as long as possible.

READ CARE INSTRUCTIONS

All yarns are not created equal. Some are extremely delicate, and others are so durable you'd think they were made of steel.

If you're giving an item as a gift, include a tag with care instructions and fiber information so the recipient knows how to wash the item correctly.

Made for you by Pam with lots of love!
This sweater is 100% wool.
Either dry clean it or hand wash it in warm water with a mild detergent. Rinse it in warm water and lay out flat to dry.

There are two terms you will see on yarn labels that usually indicate durability:

- *superwash:* This term applies to yarns made from wool, wool blends, and other animal fibers that have been chemically treated to prevent them from *felting* (shrinking and becoming very dense; for more on felting, see Chapter 5) when they are agitated in a washing machine or by hand.

- *mercerized:* This term applies to cotton that has undergone a specific chemical treatment resulting in yarn that is strong, high in luster, and takes dye extremely well.

When it comes to washing your crocheted items, be sure to follow the care instructions on the yarn label (see Chapter 1). The care instructions will tell you whether the yarn from which your crocheted item is made is machine- or hand-washable (or neither). It will also let you know if your crocheted item can be dry-cleaned and, if so, with what solvents.

STORE CROCHETED ITEMS

Store crocheted items in a clean, dry area away from pets. If the items are made of natural fibers, be sure to include cedar or lavender to repel moths and other pests that can wreak havoc on your handiwork.

chapter 7

Working from Patterns

Crochet patterns can look intimidating, but the information in this chapter will teach you how to navigate them with ease. Learn how to read crochet shorthand and how to figure your stitch and row gauge.

Abbreviations

This list is of common crochet abbreviations. For more information about some of the techniques, see Chapter 2.

Crochet Abbreviations	
Abbreviation	**Meaning**
beg	beginning
bet	between
bl	back loop
blo or BLO	work through the back loop only
BPdc or BPDC	back post double crochet
BPtr or BPTR	back post treble (or triple) crochet
CC	contrasting color
ch or CH	chain
ch-sp or CH SP	chain space
cont	continue
dc or DC	double crochet
dec	decrease
dtr or DTR	double treble crochet
edc or EDC	extended double crochet
ehdc or EHDC	extended half double crochet
esc or ESC	extended single crochet
est	established
fl	front loop
flo or FLO	work through the front loop only
FPdc or FPDC	front post double crochet
FPtr or FPTR	front post treble (or triple) crochet
FSC or fsc	foundation single crochet
hdc or HDC	half double crochet
hk	hook

Abbreviation	Meaning
inc	increase
lp	loop
MC	main color
patt st	pattern stitch
pm	place marker
prev	previous
rem	remaining
rep	repeat
rev sc	reverse single crochet (crab stitch)
rnd	round
RS	right side
sc or SC	single crochet
sk	skip
sl st, SL ST, or SS	slip stitch
sp or SP	space
st or ST	stitch
tbl	through the back loop only or through both loops, depending on the publication
tch or TCH or TC	turning chain
tfl	through the front loop only (some publications)
Tks	Tunisian knit stitch
tog or TOG	together
Tps	Tunisian purl stitch
tr or TR	treble (or triple) crochet
Tss	Tunisian simple stitch
WS	wrong side
yo or YO	yarn over

Pattern Syntax

In the interest of brevity, crochet patterns often utilize the following devices to organize instructions. With a bit of practice, you'll find that these devices make intricate patterns less wordy and easier to follow.

Parentheses ( ) and brackets [ ] are used to group sections of instructions. Often, these indicate a certain number of stitches that are to be worked into the same space, as in:

> Work [SC, CH 2, DC, CH 2, SC] into next st.

They can also indicate a small set of instructions to be repeated, as in:

> (DC2TOG over next 2 sts) twice.

Asterisks (*) are also used to group instructions. They indicate a set of instructions to be repeated a certain number of times, as in:

> SC in first st, *DC in next st, CH 1, skip 1 st, SC in next st. Repeat from * to end of row.

In this case, you would continue to repeat the "double crochet in next stitch, chain 1, skip 1 stitch, single crochet in the next stitch" until you complete the row.

Make the Cloche

Round 1: Work 8 SC into the ring; sl st into the first SC to join the round. Gently pull on the tail to tighten the ring. Mark the first st with a stitch marker and CH 2 (8 SC total).

Round 2: Work 1 ESC into the same st the Sl st is worked into. *Work 2 ESC in the next SC. Repeat from * until 1 st remains. Remove marker. Work 1 ESC in the same st the first ESC was worked into; Sl st into the first ESC to join. Place marker in the first st. Continue to move the marker to indicate the first st of every round. CH 2 (16 ESC total).

Round 3: Work 1 ESC into the same st the Sl st is worked into. Place a marker in the first st. Continue to move the marker to indicate the first st of every round. *Work 1 ESC into the next st and 2 ESC into the next st. Repeat from * until 1 st remains. Work 1 ESC into the next st. Work 1 ESC in the same st the first ESC was worked into; Sl st into the first ESC to join. CH 1. (24 ESC total)

How to Read a Pattern

At the top of a pattern, you will find information about sizing, materials, gauge, and stitch notes.

SIZING

The sizing of a garment is often indicated with the smallest size followed by larger sizes in parentheses, as shown in the figure below.

Size: small (medium, large)

Chest measurement:
32"–36" (38"–42", 44"–48")

Sizing can also be one size only, as in the pattern shown at right.

When the pattern calls for different instructions depending on size, those instructions are given in a similar fashion, with instructions for the first size followed by instructions for larger sizes in parentheses, as in:

Work 18 (20, 22) SC.

Sizing might not be indicated for some patterns, such as bags and scarves.

MATERIALS
1 hank Fleece Artist Kid Silk (70% kid/30% silk, 375 meters/250g) in Ruby Red
5.50 mm hook
Stitch marker

FINISHED SIZE
One size; 21" circumference, to fit average adult head

GAUGE
12 stitches and 13 rows = 4 inches (10 cm) in ESC

Make the Cloche
Round 1: Work 8 SC into the ring; sl st into the first SC to join the round. Gently pull on the tail to tighten the ring. Mark the first st with a stitch marker and CH 2 (8 SC total).
Round 2: Work 1 ESC into the same st the Sl st is worked into *Work 2 ESC in the next SC. Repeat from * until 1 st remains. Remove marker. Work 1 ESC in the same st the first ESC was worked into; Sl st into the first ESC to join. Place marker in the first st. Continue to move the marker to indicate the first st of every round. CH 2 (16 ESC total).

Specifications

MATERIALS
10 (**10**, **12**) balls South West Trading Company *Optimum DK* (154 yards/50g) in Silver
10 mm hook

TECHNIQUES USED
CH   Chain
SC   Single crochet
FLO   Front loop only
Using increases and decreases for shaping

FINISHED SIZE
Bust/Chest circumference S (**M**, **L**): 32–36 (**38–42**, 44–48)

Get Started
You start this sweater at the bottom of the back of the body and build out from there.
CH 38 (**44**, **52**).

CONTINUED ON NEXT PAGE

CONTINUED ON NEXT PAGE

MATERIALS

Patterns specify which yarn is called for and how much of the yarn you need. They also tell you which hook size is recommended and what notions and embellishments you need, such as yarn needles, stitch markers, or buttons.

GAUGE

Every pattern for which size is important (such as sweaters, slippers, and hats) includes information about the gauge on which the pattern is based. Always make a gauge swatch before beginning to work on such patterns so that you're sure to end up with the correct size. If your swatch is under or over gauge, adjust your hook size so that you obtain the correct gauge. (See the "Gauge" section for more information.)

Specifications

MATERIALS
1 hank Fleece Artist *Kid Silk* (70% kid/30% silk, 375 meters/250g) in Ruby Red
5.50 mm hook
Stitch marker

FINISHED SIZE
One size; 21ỉ circumference, to fit average adult head

GAUGE
12 stitches and 13 rows = 4 inches (10 cm) in ESC

Make the Cloche
Round 1: Work 8 SC into the ring; sl st into the first SC to join the round. Gently pull on the tail to tighten the ring. Mark the first st with a stitch marker and CH 2 (8 SC total).

Round 2: Work 1 ESC into the same st the Sl st is worked into. *Work 2 ESC in the next SC. Repeat from * until 1 st remains. Remove marker. Work 1 ESC in the same st the first ESC was worked into; Sl st into the first ESC to join. Place marker in the first st. Continue to move the marker to indicate the first st of every round. CH 2 (16 ESC total).

TIP

Use the gauge and yarn weight information given in the pattern to choose a yarn to substitute if you prefer not to use the yarn specified.

STITCH NOTES

Some patterns utilize stitch combinations that are complex or unique. Notes at the beginning of a pattern define the abbreviations that refer to these stitch combinations and give you the instructions once so that they don't have to be repeated throughout the pattern, as in:

> Crossed DC: Sk 1 st, work 1 DC into the next st, work 1 DC into the skipped st.

HOW TO APPROACH A PATTERN

A crochet pattern is like a recipe. Just follow the instructions one step at a time. You might find it helpful to read through the whole pattern before you begin so that you gain a better understanding of the project before you start. On the other hand, you might find the pattern less intimidating if you focus on one step at a time. Whichever way you choose, remember that the pattern is there to help you create something beautiful!

Gauge

In crochet, *gauge* (or *tension* in European patterns) refers to the number of stitches or rows in a given area of fabric.

Taking the time to measure gauge will save you from headaches and disappointment down the road by ensuring your finished project is the correct size.

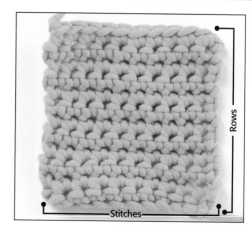

GAUGE SWATCH

Work up a gauge swatch before you begin crocheting a project. Make the swatch in the stitch pattern indicated by the pattern, so that the swatch is at least 4" by 4" in size.

Measure your gauge with a tape measure, ruler, or gauge tool. Count the number of stitches and rows to the number of inches specified in your pattern. Do not round up or down. If a stitch or row is cut off, count it as a half.

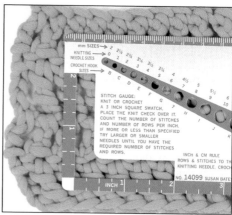

TIP

Wash and block your swatch before measuring gauge. Doing so ensures that your finished project will be the proper size after it's washed. (See Chapter 6 for more on blocking.)

Adjust Your Gauge

HOOK SIZE

If your gauge swatch has too many rows or stitches within the area specified by your pattern, swatch again with a larger hook.

If your swatch has too few rows or stitches per the unit specified, swatch again with a smaller hook.

Continue to adjust your hook size until you achieve the required gauge.

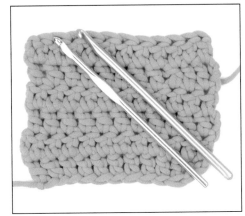

ADAPT THE PATTERN

Alternatively, you can adjust the pattern instructions to accommodate your gauge. This is especially useful if you are substituting a yarn of different weight than the one called for in the pattern. This is a simple exercise in cross-multiplication.

Take the ratio of *stitches per 1 inch/foundation chains* from your pattern (for example, 5/100), and note the ratio of *stitches per 1 inch/unknown* from your gauge swatch (e.g., 6/x). Multiply the denominator of the first ratio (100) and the numerator of the second (6) = 600. Divide the product by the numerator of the first (5); $x = 120$. Chain 120 instead of 100 to accommodate your gauge. Perform the same calculation to determine every number of stitches specified in the pattern.

Take Your Measurements

MEASURE YOUR BUST/CHEST

Standing tall, wrap a tape measure around your bust or chest at the fullest part, taking care not to wrap it too tightly. Use this measurement when deciding how much ease you would like your crocheted top to have. *Ease* is how snugly or loosely a garment fits.

If you always wear a bra under a sweater, take your measurements while wearing a bra so that your sweater will fit properly.

MEASURE YOUR WAIST

Standing tall, wrap a tape measure around the narrowest part of your natural waist, taking care not to wrap it too tightly. Use this measurement to figure how much to increase and/or decrease to shape your top at the midsection.

MEASURE YOUR HIPS

Wrap the tape measure around your hips, over the widest part of your behind. Take care not to wrap the tape measure too tightly. Use this measurement to determine how wide the bottom sweater hem should be if it is going to be long enough to cover your hips.

MEASURE YOUR ARM LENGTH

Hold the tape measure from your armpit to your cuff, with your arm slightly bent. Use this measurement to determine sleeve length.

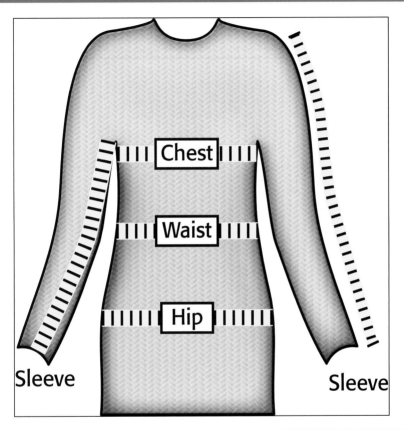

Chest

Waist

Hip

Sleeve

Sleeve

CONTINUED ON NEXT PAGE

MEASURE THE WIDTH OF YOUR BACK

Hold the tape measure from the outside of one shoulder to the outside of the other shoulder, across your back. Use this measurement to determine how wide the back of your sweater should be.

MEASURE YOUR TORSO

Hold the tape measure beginning at the most prominent bone at the base of your neck, and extend it to your natural waistline. This measurement helps you determine where to place waist-shaping in relation to the neckline.

MEASURE YOUR HEAD

Wrap the tape measure across your forehead and around the circumference of your head, keeping the measuring tape snug. Use this measurement to determine what size to make a hat.

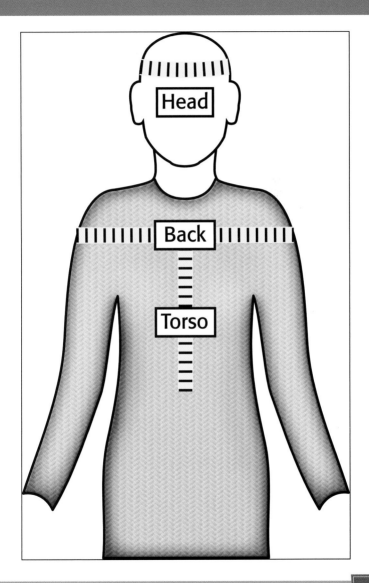

How to Read a Chart

Working with charted designs is exciting. Types of charts include color charts like this one for stranded colorwork (see page 103), filet crochet (see page 107), and tapestry crochet (see page 105).

Read the chart from right to left, from the bottom to the top, beginning at the bottom-right. Read odd rows from right to left; read even rows from left to right. If a chart refers to crocheting in the round without turning your work, all rows should be read from right to left.

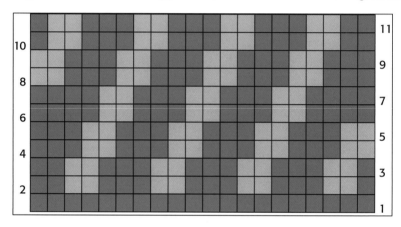

Standard Measurement Charts

The following charts are reprinted with permission from the Craft Yarn Council of America's www.YarnStandards.com.

Babies' Sizes					
Baby's Size (not age):	3 months	6 months	12 months	18 months	24 months
Chest					
Inches	16	17	18	19	20
Centimeters	40.5	43	45.5	48	50.5
Center Back Neck-to-Cuff					
Inches	10A½	11½	12½	14	18
Centimeters	26.5	29	31.5	35.5	45.5
Back Waist Length					
Inches	6	7	7½	8	8½
Centimeters	15.5	17/5	19	20.5	21.5
Across Back (Shoulder to Shoulder)					
Inches	7¼	7¾	8¼	8½	8¾
Centimeters	18.5	19.5	21	21.5	22
Sleeve Length to Underarm					
Inches	6	6½	7½	8	8½
Centimeters	15.5	16.5	19	20.5	21.5

CONTINUED ON NEXT PAGE

Standard Measurement Charts (continued)

				Children's Sizes				
Size	**2**	**4**	**6**	**8**	**10**	**12**	**14**	**16**
Chest								
Inches	21	23	25	26½	28	30	31½	32½
Centimeters	53	58.5	63.5	67	71	76	80	82.5
Center Back Neck-to-Cuff								
Inches	18	19½	20½	22	24	26	27	28
Centimeters	45.5	49.5	52	56	61	66	68.5	71
Back Waist Length								
Inches	8½	9½	10½	12½	14	15	15½	16
Centimeters	21.5	24	26.5	31.5	35.5	38	39.5	40.5
Across Back (Shoulder to Shoulder)								
Inches	9¼	9¾	10¼	10¾	11¼	12	12¼	13
Centimeters	23.5	25	26	27	28.5	30.5	31	33
Sleeve Length to Underarm								
Inches	8½	10½	11½	12½	13½	15	16	16½
Centimeters	21.5	26.5	29	31.5	34.5	38	40.5	42

Women's Sizes

Size	X-Small	Small	Medium	Large	IX	2X	3X	4X	5X
Bust									
Inches	28–30	32–34	36–38	40–42	44–46	48–50	52–54	56–58	60–62
Centimeters	71–76	81–86	91.5–96.5	101.5–106.5	111.5–117	122–127	132–137	142–147	152–158
Center Back Neck-to-Cuff									
Inches	27–27½	28–28½	29–29½	30–30½	31–31½	31½–32	32½–33	32½–33	33–33½
Centimeters	68.5–70	71–72.5	73.5–75	76–77.5	78.5–80	80–81.5	82.5–84	82.5–84	84–85
Back Waist Length									
Inches	16½	17	17¼	17½	17¾	18	18	18½	18½
Centimeters	42	43	43.5	44.5	45	45.5	45.5	47	47
Across Back (Shoulder to Shoulder)									
Inches	14–14½	14½–15	16–16½	17–17½	17½	18	18	18½	18½
Centimeters	35.5–37	37–38	40.5–42	43–44.5	44.5	44.5	45.5	47	47
Sleeve Length to Underarm									
Inches	16½	17	17	17½	17½	18	18	18½	18½
Centimeters	42	43	43	44.5	44.5	45.5	45.5	47	47

CONTINUED ON NEXT PAGE

| Men's Sizes | | | | |
	Small	Medium	Large	X-Large	XX-Large
Chest					
Inches	34-36	38–40	42–44	46–48	50–52
Centimeters	86–91.5	96.5–101.5	106.5–111.5	116.5–122	127–132
Center Back Neck-to-Cuff					
Inches	32–32½	33–33½	34–34½	35–35½	36–36½
Centimeters	81–82.5	83.5–85	86.5–87.5	89–90	91.5–92.5
Back Hip Length					
Inches	25–25½	26½–26¾	27–27¼	27½–27¾	28–28¾
Centimeters	63.5–64.5	67.5–68	68.5–69	69.5–70.5	71–72.5
Cross Back (Shoulder to Shoulder)					
Inches	15½–16	16½–17	17½–18	18–18½	18½–19
Centimeters	39.5–40.5	42–43	44.5–45.5	45.5–47	47–48
Sleeve Length to Underarm					
Inches	18	18½	19½	20	20½
Centimeters	45.5	47	49.5	50.5	52

Head Circumference						
	Infant/Child Preemie	Adult Baby	Toddler	Child	Woman	Man
Inches	12	14	16	18	20	22
Centimeters	30.5	35.5	40.5	45.5	50.5	56

8

Diagnose and Fix Problems

Everybody makes mistakes. Learn how to diagnose where things went wrong, how to correct mistakes, and how to avoid them in the future.

Recognize Extra Increases and Decreases

The best way to prevent accidental increases and decreases is to keep track of how many stitches you work in each row or round. Keep track as you go and you'll be able to catch mistakes before you've worked too far.

COUNT YOUR STITCHES

If your piece is getting narrower or wider where it's not supposed to—or if your work in the round is ruffling, curling, or buckling—count the number of stitches in the row or round and compare that number against:

- The number of stitches that the pattern or your notes say you should have.
- The number of stitches in each of the past several rows or rounds

You might find that you accidentally increased or decreased all at once or over several rows or rounds.

Note: *Remember, you can identify a stitch by its post or by the two loops that make up its top (see Chapter 2 for more on counting stitches).*

ACCIDENTALLY DECREASE?

Examine your piece to see if you skipped any stitches mid-row or -round (see photo). Hold the piece up to a light or a window and look for holes caused by skipped stitches.

SKIP THE FINAL STITCH?

Did you accidentally omit the final stitch in the previous row? This is a common mistake when you're making taller stitches because the turning chain that counts as a stitch can be easy to overlook. Take care to ensure you don't miss it.

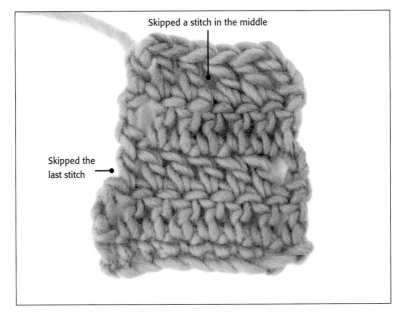

Skipped a stitch in the middle

Skipped the last stitch

CONTINUED ON NEXT PAGE

ACCIDENTALLY INCREASE?

Look for accidental increases. Did you work more than one stitch into the same stitch when you weren't supposed to?

WORK IN THE TURNING CHAIN?

Did you accidentally work into a chain from the turning chain as if it were the first stitch of the row when you weren't supposed to?

Two stitches worked into one stitch

Fix Extra Increases and Decreases

Once you have identified a mistake, choose the best way to fix it. You can rip it out, or you can compensate for it.

RIP BACK

It's easy to rip back to a mistake. If you choose to rip back, simply remove your hook from your work and tug gently on the working yarn to unravel the stitches to the error. Then reinsert your hook at that point in the pattern and rework it according to the pattern.

Note: If you rip back a significant amount, rewind the yarn so that it doesn't tangle as you rework it.

CONTINUED ON NEXT PAGE

DO A SNEAKY FIX

When the mistake is as simple as one decrease or increase, it likely won't look terrible to simply compensate for it instead of ripping out your work.

Fix by following these steps:

- Diagnose the cause of the decrease or increase so that you won't repeat it.

- Work an increase to correct an accidental decrease or a decrease to correct an accidental increase. Choose a place in the row where this correction will disappear as much as possible.

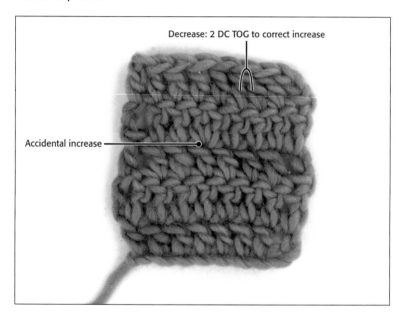

Decrease: 2 DC TOG to correct increase

Accidental increase

If Something Still Seems Wrong

If things just don't seem right with your project, take a closer look to make sure you're doing what the pattern tells you to.

CHECK YOUR PATTERN

Take a close look at the pattern's directions. Are you using the right stitch? Are you working the stitches into the correct place? Does the pattern have specific instructions to work a spike stitch, into only one loop, or around the post? Make sure you haven't overlooked a special instruction.

Did you make big changes to the type or weight of yarn suggested? If the yarn is very different from the kind used in the original pattern, be prepared for your finished product to look different.

If your work doesn't match the picture or things don't add up right, compare your work to the instructions step-by-step. If there is a mistake in the pattern, look online to see if the publisher provides a correction. If not, you may be left to your own ability to improvise. Trust your instinct or ask another crocheter for help.

CHECK WHERE YOUR PATTERN WAS PUBLISHED

If you're using a pattern published in another country, remember that they may use stitch terms differently from the way the terms are used in your own country. For example, the British and Australian *double crochet* stitch is known as a *single crochet* stitch in the United States!

US	UK
slip stitch	slip stitch
single crochet	double crochet
half double crochet	half treble crochet
double crochet	treble crochet
treble crochet	double treble crochet

> **TIP**
>
> If a step in a pattern has you stumped, try asking for help in an online message board (see Appendix). Also, check the publication's Web site to see if any corrections (known as *errata*) to the pattern have been posted.

If you find yourself getting lost in your work or you're doing complicated pattern repeats, or if you're constantly having to recount the number of stitches in a row or round, use stitch markers as guideposts. Also, if your crochet time is interrupted a lot, marked stitches will help you dive right back in where you left off.

MARK PROGRESS IN A ROW

Use stitch markers to mark your progress in long rows. For example, in a row of 100 stitches, you could mark the 20th, 40th, 60th, and 80th stitches. Not only will this make keeping track of the number of stitches easier and faster, but it will make finding accidental increases and decreases easier.

MARK REPEATS

- For a pattern that uses repeats of a complicated stitch pattern within a row, mark the end of each repeat to keep track of how many repeats you've made.

- For a pattern that repeats over a number of rows, mark the first row of the repeat sequence you are working.

Note: *You may want to make notes about what a particular stitch marker means. Clearly marking important information in your work can ease your fretting so you can get back to enjoying the project!*

Some plied yarns, as lovely as they are, can be prone to splitting while you work. Here are some tips to control this problem.

- Be gentle with your yarn. Yarn can become strained and worse for the wear if worked too tightly or handled roughly.

- Store and carry yarn in a bag to protect it from getting knocked around.

- Ripping back a project can leave yarn kinked and split; work carefully and rip back gently.

- Working tight stitches with a small hook strains the yarn. Creating loose stitches reduces the chance that you'll stab through the yarn with the hook.

TIP

It may seem that pulling a misbehaving yarn tight would be the best way to control it as you work, but pulling tight can actually cause loosely plied yarn to split.

Smooth Uneven Sides

If the sides of your work look uneven, wobbly, or squished, the problem is likely related to turning chains (see Chapter 2 for more information on turning chains).

If you make tight chains, your turning chain may not be tall enough. You might try increasing your turning chain by one chain. This only works with a very tight turning chain.

Treating a turning chain like an actual stitch can leave a gap (a) between the turning chain and the rest of the row.

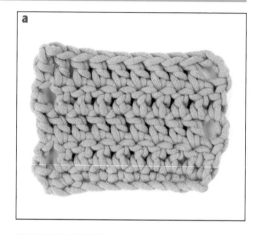

To remove this gap, work a turning chain that is one chain shorter than is usually called for. Do not skip a space; instead, work into the first stitch of the previous row. In this case, the turning chain doesn't count as a stitch (b). Experiment to see what works best for your project.

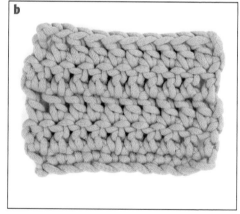

TURNING CHAIN: TO TWIST OR NOT TO TWIST

If you turn your work with the hook in the turning chain, the chain is twisted.

If you remove the hook before turning and then reinsert it, the chain is not twisted.

Each method creates a subtle difference in the sides of your work. Experiment to see which works best for you.

TIP

Remember, you can always use a simple edging to even out the sides. See Chapter 6 for more information on edgings.

Loosen Up a Tight Foundation Chain

It's important that your foundation chain isn't too tight. If it is too tight, you will have difficulty working into it. If you continue to have trouble with making loose chain stitches, try using a hook one or two sizes larger than the project calls for (remember to check your gauge on a trial swatch).

A tight foundation chain can restrict the drape and give of your fabric. If you find that your fabric needs an edge with a little extra give, try adding some extra chains throughout the foundation chain. This technique works best with mesh or lace patterns that don't use all the chains in the foundation chain. As an example, for a crocheted mesh, with 30 arches add 30 chains to the foundation chain, skip one additional chain between each arch when working the first row. Alternatively, you can use foundation stitches, which produce a much stretchier foundation than a chain (see Chapter 2 for more on foundation single crochet).

Arch mesh swatch with tight foundation chain

Mesh swatch with loose foundation chain

Fix the Fit of a Garment

As you crochet, use stitch markers to mark any increases and decreases used to shape a garment. This will help you to see where the shaping occurs so you can decide how to fix an ill-fitting garment.

If there are any areas that are simply too baggy, pinch the fabric to "take up" the excess stitches. If you pinched four stitches, try decreasing the number of stitches in that area by four.

If the shaping stitches seem out of place, you can try moving the shaping sequence over a few stitches in one direction or try starting the sequence in a different row.

You might find from a pattern's schematic that a medium bust size will fit you well, but the waist shaping of a large will make a garment that better fits your body. Do some sleuthing in the pattern to see how you might make the section of the pattern with waist shaping for the large while working with the rest of the medium instructions.

Appendix

Online Resources

The Internet offers an extensive and rapidly expanding amount of supplies and information about crochet. From patterns, yarns, and tools to message boards, magazines, and blogs, you can spend hours learning and connecting.

ASSOCIATIONS

Associations such as the Craft Yarn Council of America (CYCA) and the Crochet Guild of America (CGOA) offer resources such as tutorials, crochet-related news, and patterns.

The CYCA lists standard crochet information at www.yarnstandards.com, including hook sizes, measurements, yarn weights, and more.

The CGOA has chapters across North America; find one in your area or start one if your community doesn't have a chapter yet. The Guild hosts conferences several times a year, involving classes, a market, and an opportunity to connect socially with other crochet enthusiasts. It also has an active and thriving program for crochet professionals.

Craft Yarn Council of America
www.craftyarncouncil.com

Crochet Guild of America
www.crochet.org

MAGAZINES

Online magazines are Internet publications that publish original patterns, articles, and tutorials on their Web sites. Many print magazines offer free patterns and articles on their Web sites as well, along with additional resources only for subscribers.

Crochet!
www.crochetmagazine.com

Crochet Insider
www.crochetinsider.com

Crochet Today
www.crochettoday.com

Interweave Crochet
www.interweavecrochet.com

INFORMATIVE WEB SITES

Pioneered by enthusiastic crafters, Web sites devoted to crochet are prolific on the Web. These sites are either entirely about crochet or contain a section devoted to crochet.

Craftacular!
www.craftacular.com

Craftster
www.craftster.org

CrochetKim
www.crochetkim.com

Crochet meetups
www.crochet.meetup.com

Crochet Pattern Central
www.crochetpatterncentral.com

NexStitch
www.nexstitch.com

Stitch Diva Studios
www.stitchdiva.com

SweaterBabe.com
www.sweaterbabe.com

BLOGS, COMMUNITIES, AND CROCHET-ALONGS

A blog is an online diary or journal. The term *blog* comes from the term *Web log*. Many software programs that simplify the blogging process are available free, which means that anyone with a computer and an Internet connection can have a blog. Blog software allows readers to leave comments in response to posts, so a community can develop around blogs focusing on similar topics. Many crocheters maintain a blog devoted to their projects, displaying digital photographs of their completed projects and works in progress.

Belonging to an online community of like-minded crocheters allows for the sharing of tips, resources, advice, and often friendship. Crochet bloggers occasionally organize crochet-alongs, during with each participant works on producing an item from the same pattern or along a central theme. This allows for a fun, shared experience, and more advanced crocheters can help beginners.

Listing of Crochet Blogs
www.yarntomato.com/crochetblogs

Such Sweet Hands (Author Cecily Keim's blog)
www.suchsweethands.com

Crochet Me
www.crochetme.com

These blogs feature crochet among other inspiring craft ideas:

CRAFT Magazine's blog
www.craftzine.com

Ravelry
www.ravelry.com

Whip Up
www.whipup.net

Here are some blogging tools and other resources:

www.blogger.com

www.wordpress.com

www.livejournal.com

www.vox.com

www.slick.com (photo hosting)

MESSAGE BOARDS

Also known as forums, message boards are Web sites that organize members' comments into threads related to specific topics of conversation. General crafts-related message boards, such as www.craftster.org, contain a section devoted to crochet. Also, crochet-only message boards, such as www.crochetville.org, devote themselves entirely to crochet.

Members of a message board ask questions of the other members in hopes of finding information about techniques or to request advice. Members also share photographs of their completed crochet projects, works in progress, and links to resources they find useful. Message boards are moderated by volunteers who ensure that conversations remain polite and on topic.

Craftster
www.craftster.org

Crochetville Message Board
www.crochetville.org

Get Crafty
www.getcrafty.com

CROCHET FOR CHARITY

Many organizations distribute handmade goods to those in need. Homeless shelters, hospices, neonatal wards, disaster relief organizations, and cancer centers are only a few of the hundreds of types of groups that know how comforting a warm or cozy hat, scarf, blanket, or toy can be. Here is a short list of some organizations that are always accepting crocheted goods to distribute. If you'd like to crochet for an organization in your area, be sure to contact them first to make sure they have the resources to distribute your goods. The Crochet Guild of America has a comprehensive list of charities at www.crochet.com/charity.html.

Afghans for Afghans
afghansforafghans.org

Caps for Kids
www.geocities.com/Heartland/Hills/3272/capsforkids.html

Project Linus
www.projectlinus.org

Red Scarf Project
www.orphan.org/red_scarf_project.xhtml

Warm Up America
www.warmupamerica.com

Index

Symbols

* (asterisk) character, 164
(and) parentheses characters, 164
[and] square brackets characters, 164

A

abbreviations, crochet, 46, 162–163
acrylic fibers, 12
afghans, 128–133, 145–146
airtight bags, yarn storage, 24
alpaca, 12
angora, 12
animal fibers, yarns, 12
appliques, 116–117, 119, 121
arm length, measurements, 170–171
associations, online resources, 196
asterisk (*) character, 164

B

babies, measurement chart, 175
back, measurements, 172–173
back loop only (blo/BLO), 73–74
back porch stitch, 74
back post double crochet, 78
backstitch seam, 154
bags, 56, 105–106, 133
ball winder, 21
bamboo
   fibers, 12
   hooks, 4–5
baskets, 25, 56, 105–106
beaded yarns, 13
beads, 47, 76–87, 109
belts, fringe, 145–146
binding off, Tunisian crochet, 101
blocking, 151–152
blogs, 198
boards, blocking, 151–152
bobbles, 80
bookshelf, yarn storage, 25
borders, 75–76, 149–150
bouclé yarns, 13
boxes, triangles, 123

bracelets, children's interest, 47
broomstick loops, 110–111
bulky, yarn weight, 16
bullions, 83
bust, measurements, 165, 170
buttonholes, 136–137
buttons, attaching, 137

C

cables, 77–78
cardboard, 143–146
care instructions, 158
care symbols, 14–15
cashmere, 12
cedar chips, yarn storage, 24
center, working from, 56
center-pull skein, 19, 22
chains, motif joins, 142
chain stitch, 30–32, 36–37, 58, 61
chairs, yarn winding, 20
changing yarns, 63–64
charts, 107, 174–179
chest measurements, 165, 170
children, 47, 176
clones knot, 84–85
clusters, 79
color name/number, label, 14–15
colors, 47, 63–64, 103–106
communities, online resources, 198
corkscrews, 118
cotton fibers, 12
crab stitch edging, 149–150
Craft Yarn Council of America, 16, 175–179
crochet-alongs, 198
crochet for charity, 199
crochet in the round, 56–57
crochet on the double, 5
crochet symbols, 46

D

daisy, 116–117
decreases, 52–55, 120, 182–186
devices, pattern syntax, 164

toilet-paper roll, yarn winding, 22
torso, measurements, 172–173
toys, 56
traditional yarns, construction, 13
treble crochet, 43–44
triangles
       increase/decrease method, 120–121
       in the round, 122–123
triple treble crochet, 71
tubes, crochet in-the-round, 56
Tunisian crochet, 5, 92–102
turning chain, 33, 42, 44, 71, 184, 190, 191
twisted chains, problem solving, 191
two-ply yarns, 13

U

uneven sides, 190
United Kingdom, hook sizing, 6–9
United States, hook sizing, 6–9
unravel method, yarn estimation, 17
untwisted chains, problem solving, 191
unworked stitches, decreases, 52–53

W

waist, measurements, 170–171
wax paper, 5
weaving in, yarn ends, 66–67

Web sites, 175, 197
weight, yarn, 14, 16
wet blocking, 152
whipstitch seam, 141, 153
width of back, measurements, 172–173
winding yarn, 20–23
women, measurement chart, 177
wood, hook material, 4–5
wool, 12
woven seam, 155
wrong side, 66–67, 103

Y

yarn, winding, 20–23
yarn care symbols, 15
yarn ends, weaving, 66–67
yarn needle, uses, 11
yarn over, 29
yarns, 12–15, 17–25, 63–64, 91
yarn scraps, stitch markers, 11
yarn splits, 189
yarn weight, 16

Z

zigzags, 67
zippers, 138–139

Perfectly portable!

With handy, compact *VISUAL*™ *Quick Tips* books, you're in the know wherever you go.

978-0-470-04578-7

978-0-470-07782-5

978-0-470-09741-0

All *VISUAL*™ *Quick Tips* books pack a lot of info into a compact 5 x 7 1/8″ guide you can toss into your tote bag or brief case for ready reference.

Look for these and other *VISUAL*™ *Quick Tips* books wherever books are sold.

Read Less-Learn More®

Visual®
An Imprint of ⊕WILEY